What People Are Saying About
Master Sergeant Cedric King

"I met Cedric at Walter Reed Hospital. He was sitting in a wheel-chair with a drain hose coming out of him, having lost both legs and damaged his arm in an IED blast. He was also suffering PTSD, which affects so many of our service men and women. Despite his injuries, I was immediately taken by Cedric's spirit. There was more hope in that young man than anyone I'd ever met. I told him: 'I'm going to come back and see you.' He didn't believe me at first, but I meant it. I visited him about ten times, and we developed a friendship over the years. During one visit, I showed him a video of me snowboarding; and I said to him, 'Dude, you could do this one day.' He said, 'Even if I had the money, I could never do that.' About a year later, he agreed to join me on a ski trip to Chile. For a full week, riding in a bucket seat mounted to a Mono-Ski, Cedric tried and tried to get down the mountain. After banging himself on the ground thirty, forty times, he did it. With grace, courage, and that indomitable spirit, Cedric skied down the Andes like it was nothing. I'm in awe of this man, and proud to call him a friend."

Montel Williams

Television Personality, Radio Talk Show Host, and Actor

"For me, the best teachers and mentors are storytellers. Anyone can preach and quote doctrine from a book, but when speakers have the capacity to move an audience through their words and stories, their influence is profound. Cedric has a story of heroism, service, and perseverance. Combined together, those messages can build companies, inspire self-esteem, fix marriages, and save countries. If I could keep Cedric full-time within my organization, I would. What I have done is scheduled him often—eight speaking events in the last month alone—so his influence can be felt by many. Although he may be too humble to understand this, Cedric changes and saves lives."

Winn Claybaugh
Dean & Cofounder of Paul Mitchell Schools
Author of *Be Nice (Or Else!)*

"Cedric King is an amazing example of resilience and perseverance in the face of adversity. Wounded in Afghanistan, he's an inspiring US Army soldier who carries a message of hope everywhere he goes as he recounts his own personal journey from the loss of both legs, through the challenges faced during his rehabilitation, to his ultimate triumph over these adversities. His refusal to give up and his never-quit attitude inspire all who meet him, and I am proud and honored to have Cedric as an ambassador of the Gary Sinise Foundation."

Gary Sinise
Actor, Director, and Musician
Founder, The Gary Sinise Foundation

"He is a hero, a leader, and an inspiration."

Sean Wolfington

Chairman, Automotive Leadership Roundtable

"I still remember the first time I saw Cedric speak at a conference. He had an incredible way of inspiring the audience through his personal story and challenges. I've had him speak at two of my leadership off-sites since then, and his message still resonates and leaves me ready to take on the world. He is the model for perseverance and for believing anything is possible—in life and in business."

Thasunda Brown Duckett

CEO, Chase Consumer Banking

"Cedric's story is one of inspiration to show that one of the biggest determinants in life is not your intellect or talent, but your resilience."

Stephanie Carter

Frequent Visitor at Walter Reed National Military Medical Center along with former US Secretary of Defense, Ash Carter

THE MAKING POINT

*How to succeed when
you're at your breaking point*

CEDRIC KING

ATKINS & GREENSPAN
WRITING

The Making Point: How to succeed when you're at your breaking point
Copyright © 2019 by Cedric King. All Rights Reserved.

For more information about this title or to order other books
and/or electronic media, contact the publisher:

Atkins & Greenspan Writing
18530 Mack Avenue, Suite 166
Grosse Pointe Farms, MI 48236
www.atkinsgreenspan.com

ISBN:
978-1-945875-28-1 (Hardcover)
978-1-945875-29-8 (Paperback)
978-1-945875-30-4 (eBook)

Printed in the United States of America

Cover and Interior design: Van-garde Imagery, Inc.
Cover Image © 2013 Semper Fi Fund
Back Cover and Jacket Flap Photos © Eleven03 Photography

All photographs used with permission. All uncredited photographs
courtesy of the King Family Collection.

Dedication

I'M DEDICATING THIS BOOK to God for blessing me with this story to help heal people all over the world.

I also dedicate this book to my incredible family: the Kings, the Colemans, and the Johnsons. Without you, I would not be here, and a part of what you've put in me, shines in everything that I do, everywhere, all the time.

I love you all with every ounce of my being.

Acknowledgments

My gratitude to God is too deep to express with words; I thank Him first and foremost for this amazing opportunity to showcase his miraculous works through my life and my voice.

Secondly, I have to express immeasurable thankfulness and love to my family and friends for always being there for me, in good times and bad. I especially want to thank my wife, Khieda; our daughters, Amari and Khamya; my mother, Sandra Williams; my stepfather, Valton Williams; my sister-cousin, Jennifer Smith; and my cousin-manager, Kenya Solomon.

I love you all beyond measure.

Next, allow me to acknowledge the men and women in the military who helped me learn and grow, and who saved my life in Afghanistan, and provided support during my recovery and beyond.

Thank you to the amazing team at Walter Reed Army Medical Center; Mike Corcoran and Mike Marmolejo who got me walking; and Captain Tammy Phipps, who taught me to drive.

Immense gratitude goes to former President Barack Obama and former First Lady Michelle Obama for inviting me and my family to the White House several times after President Obama visited me in the hospital. I also want to thank former Vice President Joe Biden and Dr. Jill Biden for befriending us and including us in Thanksgiving dinner at their home. Likewise, I appreciate the support of former US Secretary of Defense Ash Carter and his wife, Stephanie Carter.

For this book, allow me to thank Starbucks Chairman Emeritus Howard Schultz and Actor/Activist Gary Sinise, founder of the Gary Sinise Foundation, for writing such eloquent Forewords to this book.

I'm also very grateful to everyone who donated time and insights for interviews; I thank you so graciously for your friendship, and most of all, for your love.

Special appreciation also goes to: former TV host Montel Williams; Carolina Panthers Coach Ron Rivera; Chase Bank Consumer Banking CEO Thasunda Brown Duckett; the Achilles Foundation; David Cordani, President and CEO of Cigna Corporation; motivational speaker Tim Storey; Automotive Leadership Roundtable Chairman Sean Wolfington; Meagan Murray from Team Velocity; photographer David Jaye; and my friend, Kelly Alston.

For the foundation and growth of my motivational speaking platform, I am forever grateful to Damon Lester, President of the National Association of Minority Automobile Dealers. Speaking opportunities with him enabled Khieda and I to meet NAMAD Founder Nathan Conyers and retired Judge Marylin E. Atkins, who introduced us to her daughters, Elizabeth Ann Atkins and Catherine M. Greenspan, who wrote and published this book through their company, Atkins & Greenspan Writing.

Elizabeth and Catherine had a way of interviewing me that created a magical synergy that awakened my absolute best ideas and stories to share in this book; the energy was so great, I tried to schedule our interviews just before my motivational speaking events because they fired me up with excitement and new messages to share on the pages of this book and with audiences across America.

Also instrumental in my speaking career has been the Andrew Gomez Dream Foundation, and for that, I thank Winn Claybaugh, Dean and Cofounder of Paul Mitchell Schools, which created the Foundation.

I could write a whole book about thanking the people who have helped me along the way. For the sake of space, I am simply going to say I appreciate you so much for all the love, support, and help with this book, with my life, with making it possible for me to help others.

Very importantly, I want to thank YOU for reading this book and using my messages to transform your breaking point into your Making Point.

Howard Schultz was an American business hero of mine long before we ever met.

First Foreword

I met Cedric King in 2014, during a visit to Walter Reed National Military Medical Center in Bethesda, Maryland. The world-class hospital and rehabilitation center treats the US military's most grievously injured, and I was touring the facility that day to learn more about the men and women who had sacrificed so very much in service to our country. Every American, especially every elected official, should visit Walter Reed. To walk its hallways and meet its residents is to see, firsthand, the tragic toll of warfare and the truest faces of bravery.

I first encountered Cedric in the cafeteria when my small group joined several of Walter Reed's patients for lunch. Whether by fate or design, I found myself sitting next to Cedric, who introduced himself and immediately began peppering me with questions. Apparently, he had read one of my books and knew a lot about my background, including growing Starbucks. I was touched by his curiosity, but it was Cedric's upbeat energy that captivated me. I wanted to know all about this soldier whose body had been torn apart but whose heart seemed intact. This man was not broken. Quite the opposite, in fact.

When I asked Cedric to tell me his story, what spilled forth was a stunning tale of heroism and humility, of profound courage, undying love of country and family, and indelible strength of character and conviction.

It is that story which fills the following pages, so I will not spoil it here. But I will say that Master Sergeant Cedric King represents not only the best of America, but the best of humankind. So moved was I by Cedric that day at Walter Reed, that I asked him if we might stay in touch, and so we began emailing. Today, I am honored to call him my friend.

Quite simply, Cedric is a force. His messages of optimism and perseverance, of faith and hard work, apply to all of us, which is why I have invited him to meet my family and speak to groups who face their own hurdles. Cedric's journey holds timeless lessons that transcend war and apply to struggles we all face. His aspirations will shock you, and no doubt inspire you.

When I first asked Cedric about the incident that cost him his limbs, he was as candid with me as he is in his book. Yet what stayed with me was his answer to my question about how he was faring now, in his fight to resume his life as a husband, a father, a son, and an athlete. Cedric replied that he believed he was a much better person because so much had been taken away from him. He had no choice, he said, but to learn to operate with less, and his life is fuller because of it.

"I wouldn't change a thing," Cedric told me.

I believe him, and so will you after reading his story.

Howard Schultz

Chairman Emeritus

Starbucks Corporation

Chatting in the shade with Gary Sinise on the set in October 2015.

Second Foreword

THERE IS A BEAUTIFUL black and white photograph of a soldier floating on his back, almost weightless in a swimming pool at Walter Reed National Military Medical Center. That soldier is missing both legs, having stepped on an IED while serving in Afghanistan in 2012. The image is tranquil, as it suggests the subject is at peace, having come to terms with his injury, ready to let God take him on the next part of his life's journey. That soldier is my inspirational friend, US Army Master Sergeant Cedric King.

In one of our early conversations, Cedric wanted to speak to me about the moment in *Forrest Gump* when Lieutenant Dan, having lost both his legs in a battle in Vietnam, finally lets go of all the anger and fear and resentment for what had happened to him and, after a smile to his friend Forrest, jumps into the calm waters of the ocean and floats on his back into the distance, finally at peace as the sun breaks through the clouds, as if lighting the way forward.

It's a beautiful part of the film, and as a double amputee, Cedric could relate. Although, I think he was also curious as to how Lt. Dan (Gary, the actor) swam on his back without using his legs when we were shooting the scene.

When Cedric first began swimming, at the encouragement of

his daughters Amari and Khamya, he said that at first it had felt like he was drowning, "…but I needed to know that I could get back to everything I did before."

My warrior friend has done that, and so much more. Quite frankly when I am around the guy I feel a little like Forrest Gump, like I should be running.

Cedric has probably run as much or more without his two legs than he did before he lost them, and certainly more than most of us. He's run marathon after marathon, competed in triathlons, all on those two blades. The Blade Runner. He never stops. Never gives up. Never quits.

He has taken what life has thrown at him and thrown it right back, I think more powerfully and beautifully than even he could have ever imagined. He is a super athlete who was a super soldier. He loves his country and he loved serving in the Army, knowing full well the risks. And this is pure Cedric King: he has compared his injury to a gift that has given purpose to his life, once saying that, "There's no reason I'm alive other than to show people the impossible really isn't impossible at all."

That's the spirit that he carries with him each and every day in everything he does. He is a devoted family man, a devoted Christian, a patriot, and a motivator who is dedicating his life to that mission, and I am honored and privileged to call him a friend. It was such a wonderful day when Cedric and his family moved into their brand new specially adapted smart technology home, built by my foundation and a team of great supporters. A great day for his family for sure. But also, a great day for all of us, knowing that we were able to give a little something back to this special family for all they have sacrificed for our country.

Cedric King is an amazing person who gave a part of himself in defense of freedom.

He would be the first to say he is not a hero. But I'll say it. He's a hero to me.

And after reading this inspirational book, I know you will feel the same way.

Cedric, thank you for sharing your story, my friend. May God continue to bless you and your family always.

Now I'm going to go running. (Just kidding.)

Gary Sinise

Actor, Director, Musician

Founder, The Gary Sinise Foundation

Preface — July 25, 2012

I AM THE CENTERPIECE of the most gruesome scene of my life.

"Thank you, Lord," I whisper.

An overwhelming feeling swells in my heart as if it's also saying, *Thank you, Lord.*

At the same time, the urge to see my wife, my daughters, and my mom burns like the fiery pain in my limbs, and howls louder inside me like the noise of 10 of these bombs going off under my feet. I need to let them know I'm okay right now.

"Thank you, Lord," I say, as my mind abandons the unimaginable pain and confusion, and I'm overwhelmed with gratitude, as if every prayer I've ever said, or that my family has spoken over me, is culminating in this unfathomable peace amidst bloody, terrifying chaos.

Introduction

HAS LIFE EVER PUSHED you to your breaking point?

Maybe you're suffering there now.

Your breaking point is where something terrible is plunging you into pain, bitterness, depression, and hopelessness. It's where you want to give up, because life doesn't seem worth living.

Your breaking point could be a health crisis, divorce, PTSD, addiction, loss of a job, death of a loved one, or any catastrophic experience.

But I'll tell you this: your breaking point is actually a gift.

Because it can actually be your making point.

That's why I named this book *The Making Point*. It symbolizes how I've transformed my thinking and my life by flipping the script on negativity into something positive.

Your Making Point can transform you into the greatest person you could possibly become.

But there's a catch.

Your Making Point will not be delivered in a pretty box with a bow on top. No, chances are, your Making Point will be obscured under trauma, tears, bandages, struggles, loss, and heartache. It will be disguised as one of the ugliest, most painful, and dreadful experiences that you don't even want to imagine.

You'll think it's your breaking point.

That's what I thought after a bomb blew off my legs in Afghanistan on July 25, 2012. I am an Army Ranger, the toughest of soldiers. I had spent 17 years cultivating mental fortitude and physical skills: jumping from airplanes, traversing mountains and swamps, and dominating physical fitness challenges. Though I started off as a regular guy who grew up with a single mom in a mobile home in North Carolina, I worked hard and never gave up. Even though it took me three tries to graduate from Ranger School in Fort Benning. (And three tries to charm my future wife into paying attention to me!) After that, I earned the rank of Master Sergeant, ultimately leading platoons through treacherous terrain as we fought the Taliban in the Middle East.

But one fateful step — and the split-second blast that followed — changed everything. I became a double amputee, undergoing countless surgeries, fearing that my wife and daughters, friends and family, would see me as less than the fun-loving father, husband, and protective provider that I had been.

I was at my breaking point.

Pain and fear sucked me into a miserable abyss that too many people — soldiers and non-soldiers alike — never escape.

But my deep faith in God was my life raft that carried me into a more glorious life than I could have ever imagined. I've befriended business moguls, professional athletes, military leaders, and many other amazing people. My wife and I met President Barack Obama and dined at the White House. I received a standing ovation from 100,000 people during the HBO Concert for Valor on the National Mall in Washington, DC. And I travel the world as a motivational speaker, sharing messages inspired by this unique story that God scripted for my life — with a surprising plot twist:

The obstacle of losing my legs was truly the greatest blessing of my life. What could have been my breaking point, actually became my Making Point.

I have learned that your weakness becomes the place where God's strength can enter and fortify you, propel you, empower you to think and act in ways that help you become your best.

Need proof? This book is full of stories that will convince you that if I, as a double amputee, can run marathons, swim, ski, drive, cycle, climb a mountain, and keep a super-positive outlook — then *you* can do anything!

So, let's start here: just 21 months after losing my legs — I ran the Boston Marathon. Wearing prosthetic legs, I was in excruciating pain by Mile 17. Seasoned runners with two natural legs call Boston's Mile 17 *the breaking point*, because it begins a grueling, five-mile stretch through Newton Hills. Its steep inclines stop some runners in their tracks. They quit right there. But somehow, the grace of God supplied me with the mental toughness to push through the physical pain, and I finished the marathon — and many others since then, including triathlons!

Demanding physical challenges such as marathons enable me to show you by example that no matter what you're struggling with right now, you already have the power inside you to change your life for the better. All you need to do is flip that "I can do it!" switch inside yourself, take action, and get ready to feel better. Fast.

In this book, I'm providing instructions on how to find your "I can do it!" switch and use all your might to turn it on. Even if it's never been activated before. There's no more time to waste being anything but your best self, no matter what you're going through. Time is our most valuable resource. We can never get it back.

If you're telling yourself that you've never been a go-getter, and all you want to do is go to work, come home, have fun on the weekend, then go back to work, you're lying to yourself. Your heart wants more out of life! More excitement, adventure, passion, and fulfillment. More of a sense of purpose and the resources to truly enjoy yourself. So I'm going to show you how to blast away whatever mental or physical obstacles are stopping you.

First, you've got an infinite power available to you 24/7. It's God. God is the engine that drives my life, my strength, my survival. Period. I view everything through a lens of gratitude to God, which enables me to expect the best, all day, every day, no matter how much agonizing pain is trying to stop me. And it's those moments when I persevere through the worst pain imaginable, that the most incredible things happen — almost instantly!

I'll tell you all about them in this book. For now, let me just say that I wrote *The Making Point* for you. It's for everyone who's seeking a spiritual path to self-help, self-motivation, and self-actualization. It is for Buddhists, Muslims, Christians, Jews, and everyone who understands that a higher power is our source of strength and miracles.

Of course, this book has a special message for soldiers who can learn how I worked hard to rise through the ranks. This story is also for veterans, to show that a fulfilling life is possible after service and devastating injuries.

This is also a love story — even a marriage manual — because it's about unconditional love for yourself and for your partner. My wife has been my saving grace. But we have witnessed many military and civilian couples split apart under the pressure of pain, trauma, and change.

This book is about leadership because it shows you that hard work, determination, and ambition pay off. This book is medicine for the mind, body, and spirit. It is a self-empowerment manual.

The bottom line is that this book is for YOU! No matter what's going on in your life, I want to help you get stronger and change yourself in ways that might seem impossible to you right now. I want you to take this information, apply it to your life, keep believing in the positive outcome you desire, and wake up one day barely recognizing your new self!

This secret to having everything you dream about in life — starting with happiness in your heart and peace in your mind — is too amazing to keep to myself. I have to share it with you and every person on the planet who wants to feel and live better.

So, I invite you to read on, and learn how I choose to do this every single time, whether I'm keeping a faithful and cheerful spirit despite searing pain while standing in line at the airport, or whether I'm summoning every ounce of mental and physical strength to push through Mile 17 of the Boston Marathon.

I know that if I can do it, you can, too.

I also know that you don't have to get your legs blown off to struggle with your own breaking point. You might be suffering in your marriage or relationship or with your kids or family. You might be battling an addiction or agonizing over your health or weight. You might have a passion for something completely unrelated to your current job, relationship, or lifestyle, but making the change would require taking great risks. Risks your family or friends may not support. But your current situation may be killing you inside.

Your heart may want something, but your head is saying, *No, that's not attainable!*

My mission right now is to help you find your Making Point.

It might be the toughest thing you'll ever do, but it's worth its weight in gold. So, if you'll use this book as your how-to guide to transform your breaking point into your Making Point, I promise that you will rise up and out of the sadness, the fear, the gloom and doom, and become your best YOU!

MSG Cedric King (Ret.)

Contents

1

Discovering Your Making Point

I'M JOLTED FROM SLEEP by the long, deep drone of the Muslim call to prayer in Arabic over a loudspeaker far above my tent. Here on the US Army Forward Operating Base in one of the most dangerous parts of Afghanistan, the man on the amplifier chants every morning at 0500 hours:

"Aaaaaaaaallllllllaaaaaaaaahuuuuuuuu Aaaaaaakbaaaaaar," over and over, followed by the prayer.

This almost-haunting sound pulls me from my own prayerful dreams about good times back home with my wife and two small daughters. I picture them in my mind every night as I go to sleep, and they are my first thought in the morning.

But Khieda, Amari, and Khamya seem a million miles away from the war zone where I'm waking up to the task of leading the 32 men of 3rd Platoon across bomb-rigged ground, into enemy-infiltrated villages, and through Taliban shoot-outs, as I've done every day for the past five months of my deployment.

"Thank you, Lord," I pray silently, grateful for the safety of my family and the 80 Alpha Company soldiers here at the HR2 camp in volatile Kandahar Province. I stay in prayer all day and even in my

1

sleep, feeling shielded by the prayers of my wife, my mom, and our extended family as my men and I endure the scorching desert heat and intense, continuous danger.

My eyes open in the dark tent, as the 15 men on nearby cots rustle awake. The dry air stings my eyes, and I'm hit with the dusty, gunsmoke smell of war in Afghanistan. My mind fast forwards through the day ahead.

It's Wednesday, July 25, 2012, the sixth day of Ramadan, the holiest time of the year for Muslims. But that hasn't slowed the insurgents' assaults. During the past five days, more than a dozen NATO troops and contractors have been killed in Afghanistan, emphasizing what has already been a vicious and deadly summer.

The *rat-tat-tat!* of insurgents shooting at us is a constant, wicked lyric in the soundtrack of our days.

Because we are light infantry, we walk everywhere. We do this knowing that every step could be our last, because we're living in a minefield. Improvised Explosive Devices are buried under the roads where we drive, on the routes where we walk, and in the primitive mud-and-straw buildings that we search. These IEDs or "dirty bombs" are the Taliban's favorite weapon. They're covered with pressure plates that are set off by a footstep or a vehicle's wheel.

These IEDs — sometimes made of old mortar rounds and filled with explosive fertilizer along with scraps of glass and metal intended to shred flesh — have cost our senior medic his leg and have injured several others from Alpha Company. Before summer's end, IEDs and gunshots would give rise to 20 of us receiving Purple Heart medals honoring battle-fallen soldiers.

We've had so many injuries, it's been difficult to call home. Every time a soldier is hurt or killed, a black-out blocks the phone lines, so no bad news can leak out before the military contacts the wounded soldier's family. Unfortunately, that's made it hard to talk to Khieda and the girls. And just a week ago, when I did get to call, I learned of my eight-year-old daughter Amari's nightmare: she saw me lying on the ground here, injured.

"Baby girl, Daddy is doing fine," I told her during a brief chat as other soldiers waited to use the phone behind me. "Nothing is going to happen to me. I'll be back in no time."

I realized that I was telling her this from a combat zone rife with shootings, explosions, and anarchy. But for me, it was like calling home from the office. The battlefield was my chosen place of employment, and I was as certain as any accountant or computer analyst that I would go home when my work was done. So, I promised my daughter: "Amari, we're going to Disney World when I come home."

"Okay, Daddy."

When I hung up, I didn't worry about any prophetic power in my daughter's bad dream. Nor did I once consider that I would get hurt.

Back to the moment when I'm waking up in Afghanistan: the man on the loudspeaker continues his chant: "Allahu Akbar, Allahu Akbar." I sit up on my cot and slip my feet into my combat boots; this act signals my brain and body to jump into action.

At the same time, the Afghan National Army soldiers who are embedded among us kneel on their mats and pray. We're here as part of the Army's 82nd Airborne Division to help stabilize the Afghan government, just a year after American soldiers killed Osama bin Laden in retaliation for the September 11, 2001 attacks.

We live under the constant threat of Taliban attacks, and we've developed some unique defense tactics that include candy and Cracker Jacks. No joke, these treats sent in care packages from my wife, mother, and other relatives have saved me and my platoon more times than I can count. The Taliban doesn't usually attack when children are around us, so I always keep treats in my pockets. When the kids see me coming in their villages, they know I have something for them. As a result, children cluster around us. Amazingly, in exchange for a box or two of Cracker Jacks sent by my Uncle Chuck or Aunt Karen, the kids even lead us to places where bombs are camouflaged — and tell us where the insurgents live!

Today we will not have such protection or help from children. We'll be doing a reconnaissance on a nearby village that became so dangerous, the villagers abandoned it. Not only is it rigged with IEDs, but anyone who approaches this village will be attacked by gunmen.

Am I scared? No! I signed up for this, and I love it. In fact, when I first joined the Army right out of high school, I took a desk job, thinking it would be safe and comfortable. I hated it! I craved adventure and excitement. I wanted battlefield action!

So, I volunteered for the United States Army Ranger Course in the rugged environment of Fort Benning, Georgia; Dahlonega, Georgia; and Eggland, Florida. Ranger School was so mentally and physically grueling, I flunked out the first two times. But I never gave up. I swam through ice-cold swamps, climbed mountains, underwent food and sleep deprivation, and experienced life-and-death training scenarios in the wilderness.

Finally, on my third try, my hard work and persistence paid off. I became the bearer of a Ranger tab on my uniform. It's the mark of an elite soldier, the toughest of the tough, ranked up there with the Navy Seals and Green Berets.

I'm also a paratrooper, and I've jumped out of airplanes 92 times after completing Army Airborne School at Fort Benning, Georgia.

That might sound petrifying, but I love it. Throughout the whole experience, I felt protected by God, and exclaimed, "Thank you, Lord," every time I jumped out of a plane and landed safely on the ground. Always seeking the next level of adventure and achievement, I graduated the US Army Jumpmaster Course, the Pathfinder Course, and the Air Assault Course. In fact, I've graduated from all but one of the Army's leadership training courses!

So now, being in threatening territory in Afghanistan is exactly where I belong. It's my job, and I love it. I'm aware of the risk, but I don't get scared, and I march through each day defeating the enemy while knowing that God will take me home. I now have the confidence and courage that I lacked as a little kid growing up with a single mother in a trailer in Norlina, North Carolina. Back then, two bullies used to beat me up on the school bus. I was scared, and I did not fight back. In fact, I was a low achiever all the way around. My grades hovered around Cs, Ds, and Fs; I wasn't even good at the sport that I loved: basketball.

Despite all this, my mother, Sandra Williams, began planting seeds in my mind and heart, starting as early as I can remember. Sometimes daily, sometimes weekly, she'd say, "I don't know what it is, but God has something in mind for you. You were meant to do something very special." I didn't know what she meant, and I saw no evidence that her words would ever come true. But she believed and repeated these words over me so many times, I believed her.

Meanwhile, I hated being afraid of bullies. I also hated struggling at something that my hero, Chicago Bulls superstar Michael Jordan, made look so graceful and powerful. So, I mustered up some strength from deep inside, and practiced hoops for hours and hours and hours by myself on a bumpy, dirt "court." I shot my basketball into a bottomless plastic milk crate nailed to a tree as a makeshift hoop — until I finally made the varsity team at Warren County High School. After that, as people cheered for me on the court, the bullies left me alone.

Years later, the Army continued to teach me to conquer fear by developing the mental and physical strength to fight back. Now I'm 6'2" of solid muscle, always scoring a perfect 300 in Army physical fitness tests, and working out all the time here on the outpost.

So, if anybody is ready for a fight and a tough assignment in a battle zone, it's Master Sergeant Cedric King. That's why I was unfazed last night when our commander gave me and Lieutenant Jake Kohlman the order for today's mission: bring back evidence that the Taliban is building bombs in a nearby village. The village in question is unfamiliar to us, so we decide to buck our usual *modus operandi* of alternating leadership on daily village patrols. Usually, Lieutenant Kohlman leads one, and I lead the next. Today, we're doing this one together.

On top of that, the last-minute nature of this assignment inspired us to proceed with extra caution, as our commander called on our platoon to cover for another that was supposed to take this mission. But something came up, prompting a sudden change of plans.

When a US Army commander gives an order, you follow it. I had not earned my leadership role on the battlefield by questioning decisions, including signing a waiver to go on this deployment so soon after my 2011 deployment to Afghanistan. My dwell time at my home station in the states had been only six months; in fact, I had only received my physical papers for this deployment on the morning that I left home.

I had risen through the ranks by meticulously following orders and protocols to execute every mission with excellence and precision.

While doing so, protecting my platoon's safety is a top priority. That was the case during my first deployment to Iraq in 2003, as well as during my second in Afghanistan, and it continues on this day.

DEPLOYMENTS

I was deployed to Afghanistan in 2011 as well as Iraq in 2003 before my third deployment to the Middle East when I was injured on July 25, 2012.

This was one of the toughest times to say goodbye to Khieda and our daughters before I left on my third deployment to the Middle East.

Now, I head out into the dark morning with my shave kit, and brush my teeth with bottled water. The outpost has no running water, so the only way to take any semblance of a shower is to hang a water bottle upside down with a piece of cord and punch holes in the cap. As for the bathroom, we use rustic outhouses containing modified 55-gallon drums for toilets.

We get three meals a day, but one is an MRE, or Meals Ready to Eat, which is freeze-dried food such as beef stew, veggies, and my favorite: chicken and salsa. Add water to this little heat pouch, which warms your "little brown bags of goodness" as we called them, and that's the meal. On the rare occasions that I ate breakfast, I'd have a ramen noodle bowl sent by Khieda.

On this day, I skip breakfast. Then comes my gear: helmet, gloves, eye protection, and my bulletproof vest. The vest weighs nearly 50 pounds after I load up my body armor, which contains 10 magazines of 30 bullets each. I also bring the two bottles of water that I'd put in the refrigeration unit the night before so they are now solid blocks of ice that will thaw as we trek to the village. That's my big thing: cold water for the walk.

As I get prepared, I feel more than ready to go home to my family. I admitted this in recent emails to my wife, my mom, my grandparents, and dozens of aunts, uncles, and cousins who pray constantly for divine protection over me and my platoon. I know that they all play a major part in keeping us safe from the enemy.

I always feel God's shield around me. I grew up in the First Baptist Norlina Church, and was even the "superintendent" of Sunday school with my cousin Jennifer, who is the same age as me and was my constant companion as a child. This tough time in Afghanistan has only strengthened my strong faith and relationship with God.

"This time of testing," I wrote in a July 3, 2012 email to my family, "has truly shown me more than at any other time, that prayer does work. This experience has taught me that prayer is one of the many weapons that God has given us to have dominion over this realm, just as he has told us to have."

This photo was taken of me on July 24, 2012, the day before an IED blasted off my legs in Afghanistan.

Before I left, my mom gave me Psalm 91 — the go-to Psalm of her grandmother Margaret — and ordered me to read it and speak it every day. Sometimes I study it and other scripture at night in my tent while munching on the Oreos, Poppycock, and Gardetto's that she and Khieda send in weekly care packages. All the while, I obeyed my mother's orders to meditate on Psalm 91. Some of my favorite lines include:

> *Thou shalt not be afraid for the terror by night;*
> *nor for the arrow that flieth by day;*

Nor for the pestilence that walketh in darkness;
nor for the destruction that wasteth at noonday.

A thousand shall fall at thy side, and ten thousand at thy right
hand; but it shall not come nigh thee.

There shall no evil befall thee, neither shall any plague come
nigh thy dwelling.

For he shall give his angels charge over thee, to keep thee in all
thy ways.

They shall bear thee up in their hands, lest thou dash thy foot
against a stone.

For some reason, the words "dash thy foot against a stone" resonate with me in this land where every step on the ground could set off a bomb.

Because of the extreme danger of today's mission, and our unfamiliarity with the village, Lieutenant Kohlman and I hope that by leaving early, we can get out and avoid a Taliban attack. Plus, it's going to hit 120 degrees by 11:00 a.m., with a hot, dry wind blowing up dust and sand. The earlier we get moving, the better.

We review the game plan, starting with a mission briefing that includes the five W's: Who, What, When, Where, and Why. Our chances for success are greater if everybody knows every detail of the plan. After the five W's, we load up on ammo. Then we do our spot check.

"Jones, Ramirez, Santiago, come over here," I say. As the three soldiers stand in front of me, I order, "Show me your canteens and your third magazine of ammo. And let me see your left canteen."

They do as told.

"Santiago, where are we going?" I ask.

"We're going to this village," he says, describing our mission.

I check the ammo they've loaded, and make sure they've got a good supply of water. Everyone is good to go. But before leaving the outpost, Lieutenant Kohlman and I do a headcount. We stand facing each other as the soldiers walk single file between us at the gate. I'm counting; he's counting.

With us are Sergeant Chris Anayannis, who's carrying the Skedco stretcher, and two new soldiers, Esteban Reyes and Medic Aaron Keller, whose medic pack contains first aid supplies in case anyone is injured. After everybody has gone through, I announce the number of soldiers I counted: "Thirty-eight."

Then Lieutenant Kohlman states his headcount: "Thirty-eight."

PLATOON: This was my third time leading a platoon in the Middle East on missions under the blistering heat and gunfire from insurgents. In this July 4, 2012 photo, just weeks before my injury, that's me standing on the far left as the leader of about 30 soldiers in the Alpha Company 3rd Platoon, the first of the 508th Parachute Infantry Regiment.

Our numbers match, so I call the camp base and tell them we are heading out, including the number of Afghanistan National Army

(ANA) soldiers accompanying us. As we walk away from the outpost, the sun comes up. It's already in the low 80s. In my right hand, I carry an M4 carbine rifle with 5.56 mm bullets. Walking through desert heat under a helmet, uniform, and 50 pounds of gear can zap your energy quickly. But we're ready for it: we work out every day at the outpost.

Each platoon carries two light submachine guns and a heavy machine gun. The ANA soldiers carry machine guns, too. We're heavily armed. Safety is rule number one; we practice muzzle awareness by keeping our weapons pointed toward the ground.

FOOT PATROLS: My platoon conducted patrols along bomb-rigged, gravel roads like this throughout the desert of Afghanistan as we went on daily missions. That's me in the middle.

As we walk, I know beyond all reasonable doubt that this is where I'm meant to be at this moment. I've been in the Army for 17 years, and I love my job. I always prefer being on foot. Light infantry is gritty and rough. On foot, I know if we get into a shoot-out with some bad guys, I can take care of myself and get out of any situation. It's all about the Army acronym SURVIVAL:

BUILDINGS: I stepped on a "dirty bomb" inside a structure similar to the one behind these soldiers. With thick mud walls hardened by the hot sun, these huts are typical of villages in Afghanistan.

S — Size up the situation

U — Use all your senses / Undue haste makes waste

R — Remember where you are

V — Vanquish fear and panic

I — Improvise

V — Value living

A — Act like the natives

L — Live by your wits, but for now learn basic skills

Trusting my ability to survive under any circumstances engenders trust among the soldiers in my platoon. We are nothing without each other's trust. Our lives are literally in each other's hands.

Years earlier, my buddy came under attack and almost lost his leg. He had described Afghanistan to me before I'd come here. He told me that some of the most courageous guys would be terrified to do these village patrols on foot. I remember from that moment on, I had always prayed for strength and courage when the time came for me to be a leader. I probably made that prayer for two or three years, and when the moment arrived, I was not once scared. I never thought, *I don't want to go out there*. I had no fear of problems. I was so sure I would be okay.

On this fateful day, as always, I count my paces to keep track of the distance travelled and the distance to our destination. About 500 yards from the outpost, we're walking through nine-foot tall grass to cross a huge marsh.

Rat-tat-tat!

Shots. We hit the ground. It's a soldier's instinct: get low. Coming under fire is normally not a big deal. It's just part of the job. The tall grass conceals us, but it's actually an obstacle. It hinders us from seeing our targets.

These guys have one MO: they're just shooting at the grass, figuring they'll hit someone, and hoping that if they do, they'll disrupt and disorient us.

But they don't.

Despite our problematic vantage point for fighting back, we succeed, unscathed, and quickly get back on track, walking toward the village. Because the ground is infested with IEDs, we're careful to walk in line and step in the footsteps of the person ahead of us. The next 1,000 yards go by quickly. We cross a stream that's about chest deep. The water feels good, but there's a current and a steep bank on the other side, so we each must pull out the guy behind us.

Reyes, who's only been with the platoon four or five days, yanks me out of the water. This is his first foot patrol, and he's just experienced his first shoot-out. I know this might be scary for him, and I want to make it as comfortable as possible, and let him know it will be okay.

As he lifts me and my 50 pounds of gear up and out of the water onto the bank of the stream, I say, "You good?"

"Yeah, Sarge. I'm good."

"Just stay calm," I tell him. "Be cool."

No sooner than we're all out of the stream, we're attacked again.

I get a call that the bad guys are in a hut — a sun-baked, mud-and-straw type of structure with eight-inch-thick walls, a typical building for the region. The guys attacking us don't want us to reach the hut. These guys are well-fortified from their position because shooting at those huts is like firing at sandbags. Bullets don't penetrate the walls.

Our soldiers are on the outer perimeter, staying low.

"Don't panic," I say. "Just shoot back at those shooting at you."

Sergeant Chris Anayannis, who's carrying the Skedco stretcher, is walking with us. He assures Reyes that we'll be fine.

"The spray-and-run tactics of the attackers are no big thing for us," Sergeant Anayannis says. "The guy who shoots off 10 to 15 rounds over a wall is just taking pot shots to try to stir us up. He's less of a threat than an ambush."

When we reach a deserted hut, and we know that the road is full of IEDs, our engineers set off several controlled detonations. If any IEDs are in our path, these deliberate explosions will set off the dirty bombs, clearing the way for us to pass safely.

"Three, two, one, detonate!" our men shout.

Bam!

The explosions begin. Our soldiers are also shooting back at attackers who are firing at us from behind a wall. At the same time, our team sets off another controlled explosion.

"Three, two, one, detonate!"

Bam!

Meanwhile, I want to enter the hut, but not through the doorway. That's the obvious place where IEDs are hidden, so we never enter through the doorway. Instead, our engineers build a charge, and *Bam!* They blow a hole in the wall, and we enter through it. The interpreter and a few other soldiers join me. We're looking around.

Now inside the hut, I'm overwhelmed with an eerie feeling. It's deserted, with little hallways and an interior courtyard surrounded by a seven-foot wall. In the main room, which is about 15 by 20 feet, mats are laid out on the floor; they're big enough for a person to outstretch for prayers. Sunlight pours through the door and the blast hole.

Yes! We hit the jackpot. The Afghan rebels are definitely using this place to build primitive bombs. It's full of all the ingredients needed to make dirty bombs, including: fertilizer; mixing tubs; wires from lamps, refrigerators, and heaters; batteries; and pieces of glass, nails, screws, rocks, and metal used for shrapnel.

We've found their weapons cache. I walk around for a minute or two, looking at everything. Then I go outside, and come back in. All of us are stepping on the same spots on the dirt floor, sometimes crossing the same place two, three, four times...

Baaaaaammmmm!

A blast under my foot propels me upward.

I'm airborne — in a huge cloud of dirt.

A sound louder than jet engines blasts my ears.

Burning pain, as if I'm tossed into a fire, assaults my body.

I gasp for breath.

My body slams into the hole that the bomb blasted in the dirt floor.

I'm on my back. Dust rains down on me.

"Thank you, Lord," I say, as if I'd just jumped out of an airplane and landed safely. I've seen thousands of IED explosions, been awakened in the middle of the night by them, and I'm still surprised by the force and noise of this blast.

Still, my first thought is, *It can't be that bad.*

So, I try to stand up. My Army Ranger fighter instinct tells me: *You got knocked down. Now you get up.*

I keep trying to stand up, but I keep falling down.

Suddenly our platoon medic, Aaron Keller, is over me. He yells: "Just stay down!"

I read his lips because the blast has muffled my hearing. I trust him, so I stop trying to get up.

The room is cloudy with dust everywhere. Five other men are down, moaning in pain, on the floor around me. Radios crackle with urgent commands:

"Somebody's hit! Skedco!"

"Keep pulling security! Keep your eyes open!"

I smell burning flesh.

Then I look down at my body.

The force ripped my rifle from my right hand. It now lies bent like a banana, and by the grace of God, it did not fire. Nor did the blast ignite the 300 bullets attached to my vest. In a split second, I acknowledge that life-saving miracle.

I look at my right arm: I can see straight through it. The bones of my forearm are exposed. I can see my pulse. The tissue is rising and falling in the meat inside my wrist. Blood is gushing from the artery in the small of my elbow joint.

That's the nuttiest thing. It looks like anatomy class.

The chest plate in my bulletproof vest is cracked. Blood is everywhere — squirting from my arms and my legs. My legs look like hamburger meat. My left heel is on the ground but the arch of my foot is facing the ceiling.

I am the centerpiece of the most gruesome scene of my life.

"Thank you, Lord," I whisper.

An overwhelming feeling swells in my heart as if it's also saying, *Thank you, Lord.*

At the same time, the urge to see my wife, my daughters, and my mom burns like the fiery pain in my limbs, and howls louder inside me like the noise of 10 of these bombs going off under my feet. I need to let them know I'm okay right now.

"Thank you, Lord," I say, as my mind abandons the unimaginable pain and confusion, and I'm overwhelmed with gratitude, as if every prayer I've ever said, or that my family has spoken over me, is culminating in this unfathomable peace amidst bloody, terrifying chaos.

My daughter's nightmare comes to mind. She woke up screaming, telling her mom she'd seen me lying on the ground, injured. Now I'm lying on the ground, with my see-through arm, my minced legs, my mangled foot. And I'm waiting for the angels to come get me, still saying with my breath and my heart, *Thank you, Lord.* Over and over and over. I start wondering which line I'll be in when I reach the Pearly Gates. If I see Hitler or Saddam Hussein in my line, I'll be worried.

"Ahhhhhrrrrgggggggg!" I yell. I'm making grunting sounds, because the shrapnel has ripped through me, and everywhere hurts, burns, stings. My hand throbs like someone is slamming it with a hammer.

"What kind of pain are you in?" Doc Keller asks as he tightens tourniquets on all four limbs.

I feel calm as the blood stops squirting and someone calls for a Medevac, the helicopter that will take me and the other injured soldiers to the nearest base for treatment.

"It could be worse," I tell Doc Keller as he's working on me. "We could be back in that grape row doing 10,000 air squats to keep warm."

He smiles, laughs. "We spent three days out there," he says. "Satan's inferno during the day, and the bottom drops out at night."

In the middle of this chaos, I am cracking jokes, trying to ease the tension of this deadly situation for the others and myself. Remembering the time we were stuck in the grape row — a sort of primitive vineyard — with nothing to fight the cold of the desert night but our own body movement, seems like a worse situation than this. I'm just trying to pass time.

"The bird's inbound," someone says.

When the Medevac arrives, about 25 minutes have passed, and we're still under fire. An Apache helicopter accompanies the Medevac. No bad guy is going to try to attack this tank in the sky.

I'm rushed to the Medevac. My medical evacuation priority is "urgent, surgical." In other words, *You've got two hours to get this guy to the hospital; fatality is imminent.*

All my guys are around me, escorting me to the helicopter. They want to help me, which I appreciate, but the shoot-out is ongoing. Even though it's not heavy fire, they still have a job to do, whether I'm there on the ground with them or not. I can't let them lose focus, even if I am on a stretcher with my legs zig-zagging in every direction and hanging on by threads of tissue.

I spring into maniac Master Sergeant mode, barking orders: "Stop paying attention to me! Turn around! Pull security!"

I wave my one good arm for emphasis. "Get out there and pay attention to the battle space! Stop paying attention to me! Pull security on the perimeter!"

I say to Lieutenant Kohlman, "Look, take care of the boys. Bring them home safely. Make sure they go to Ranger School. I'll be alright."

As I'm being lifted into the Medevac, Lieutenant Kohlman jumps into action. And I know they will be alright. I can stop giving orders now.

"Thank you, Lord," I say. I think of Psalm 91, and how I had struck my foot against a stone in the form of an IED.

As the bird speeds toward Kandahar Army Airfield, the medics give me a morphine lollipop. It numbs my pain, except for the burning in my upper thighs from the shrapnel. Doc Keller's tourniquets are keeping my blood in my body.

And suddenly I am simultaneously questioning how long I have to live and yet knowing with absolute certainty that I will see Khieda and the girls. I am not scared. Deep in my heart, I know that I will be okay.

But my body is telling a different story. It's difficult to breathe, because I have a collapsed lung. I am no longer cracking jokes or giving orders when I am rushed into the medical hospital on the largest air base in Afghanistan. My blood pressure plunges so low that doctors immediately put me into a medically induced coma. This saves my life, which has suddenly become an episode of *M*A*S*H*, the 1970s TV show series about a military medical unit during the Korean War.

While I am deep in the coma, doctors amputate my foot. Then my leg. Then the other leg. As I hover at death's door, I am too fragile to be flown out of Afghanistan to Landstuhl Regional Medical Center in Landstuhl, Germany, my first stopover before I can come back stateside.

I was injured around 10 in the morning, which was 12:30 in the morning North Carolina time. Seven-and-a-half hours after that IED made me go airborne, Khieda gets a call. In her words…

I got the call at eight in the morning. I didn't have to be at work until later. The gentleman on the phone tells me his name and that he has some bad news.

"Sergeant First Class King has been severely injured in Afghanistan," he says.

"What? What do you mean he got injured?"

"He stepped on an IED," he says. "His left foot has been amputated below the ankle. And his right leg is severely injured. Ma'am, his condition is very serious."

I'm panicked. I'm starting to cry. Everything else this guy is saying sounds like Charlie Brown's teacher.

"I have to tell his mother!" I shriek.

"Ma'am, that's my next call."

I am grateful for this. I can't tell his mom. Cedric is her only child. I can't make that call.

He gives me an 800-number to call for updates. I'm heaving. I'm hysterically crying. I send the kids next door.

Meanwhile, I'm still days away from coming back into the land of the conscious, and my mom is getting the same call that Khieda received. In my mom's words…

My husband, Valton, answered the phone when it rang around 8:15 in the morning. He hands me the phone, and says, "The Army is calling."

I'm thinking, "What achievement has my son earned this time?" As I take the phone, I'm expecting congratulations. Little did I know, my son had, in fact, received two very important honors: the Purple Heart and the Bronze Star.

"Ms. Sandra Williams?" says the gentleman on the phone.

"Yes, this is she."

"Ms. Williams, we have to inform you that Sergeant King has been severely injured and is in critical condition."

"WHAT DID YOU SAY?"

"Sergeant King has been severely injured and is in critical condition."

The room starts spinning around me. I shout, "IS HE ALIVE?"

"Yes, ma'am."

I ask if Khieda knows. He says yes, then starts giving me a number to call for updates on Cedric's condition. I'm trying to write, but my whole being is rattled; I can't remember how to write the number three. I turn to Valton and ask, "How do you make a three?"

At that point, Valton takes the phone and gets the number, and hangs up.

By now, the entire house, not just the room, is spinning. I call Khieda.

From the sound of our conversation, anyone would have thought we were speaking an unknown tongue through our sobs and wailing mixed with incoherent words and attempts at communicating. My very strong, stable-minded husband took the phone from me and said, "Khi, we're on our way to you."

I am too upset to call Dad and Mother, so I try my sisters. Crying hysterically, I finally get hold of my older and ever-calm sister Corlis, who says, "Sandra, he is alive. He's healed and he's whole."

"I know, I know," I say.

"You need to speak that," she says. "Speak it."

"I know, I know. I know, I know."

Then she screams, "Speak it now!"

"He's healed and he's whole!" I say again and again.

She returns to a calm demeanor and says she'll notify the rest of the family.

When we get to Khieda's, Amari greets us and says, "Granny, Daddy is alive, he survived!"

From the mouths of babes! That calms me down for a second, but updates continue to come in. Cedric's left leg has been amputated. He still has his right leg.

We stayed most of the day, then Valton and I went back home. Our phone was like Grand Central Station, keeping every relative informed of Cedric's condition as we got updates.

Shortly after we're back from Khieda's, I watched Valton answer the phone.

As he listened, he grabbed the countertop. Then he started crying, bawling.

From Valton's reaction, I think Cedric has died. I start screaming, "NOOOOOOO, GOD, NOOOOO! YOU CAN'T TAKE MY BABY! YOU CAN'T! GOD, DON'T TAKE MY BABY!"

I come to as Valton is splashing water on my face. He tells me they had to take Cedric's other leg, and soon they will be able to transport him home. That scare really shook me up. In the middle of the night, I went into the den, fell on my knees and asked, "GOD, WHY CEDRIC?"

I heard in my spirit: "Why not? Your family is not immune from this. Who else could better show my glory in this than Cedric?"

My loved ones are suffering, I'm losing limbs, but I'm still in a coma. I am finally stable enough to fly by Medevac to Walter Reed National Military Medical Center in Bethesda, Maryland. A crew of people greets us, including a Red Cross Volunteer named Dr. Joan Gordon. The strength and faith of this stranger is like a tow rope pulling me up the side of a very challenging mountain until my wife and mom arrive to get me all the way to the peak.

In Ms. Joan's words…

Cedric arrived in the Medevac, with aides and attendants surrounding him on a gorgeous, sunny day. My duties as a volunteer were to greet the Medevac team, bring them bags of goodies, snacks. From his condition, all the equipment, and the incredibly attentive staff members who were assigned to get him into the hospital, I was concerned about him.

I did a quick prayer then. I said silently, "God, if it be your will, let him live." That night I awoke at two in the morning and started praying for him again. I was one of the first people stateside to pray for him. God placed these thoughts in my mind and I acted without questioning it, though it was certainly outside my volunteer duties.

The next time I volunteered, I saw him, still in a coma, before his wife and mother arrived.

I said to him as he lay there, bandaged and unconscious: "God's light is going to shine through you. God has a special assignment for you, and that's why he's chosen you to go through this. You are going to motivate others."

Ms. Joan's fateful words did not fall on deaf ears.

Around the time I was arriving at Walter Reed, my mother-in-law, Patricia Jackson-Holley, was losing her job outside Tacoma, Washington. This might seem like an obstacle, but it was a blessing. She was flown down to Fayetteville to watch the girls while Khieda and my mom came up to wait for me to wake up. In Khieda's words…

Before we went up to Walter Reed, I was at one of my lowest points. I was so devastated. I could barely sleep. I wasn't eating. I had been packing, and I just walked out of the house in my socks and started to walk around the cul-de-sac.

Clear as a bell, I hear the words, "I'm still me."

It was Cedric. Our spirits had connected in that moment across the thousands of miles separating us.

I went back in the house and got ready to go.

The girls knew Dad was hurt, but they didn't know he'd lost his legs. My mom stayed with them in North Carolina to keep things relatively normal while Cedric's mom and I traveled to Walter Reed. An escort and a liaison picked us up from the airport.

We were briefed on what to expect. We checked into our hotel and then were taken to Walter Reed. As we drove up, I'm thinking, this hospital is so massive; how are we going to figure this out? I knew we would, as we had done with every new base, every new job.

We get to his floor. I pause; I can't go straight in, so our liaison, Sergeant Jackson, takes us into a little family waiting room where we hold hands and say a prayer.

"Okay, time to go in," Sergeant Jackson says. "Put your game face on. He needs to see you the way he has always seen you. If you go in there and panic, he's going to panic."

I determine then and there that I'm not going to cry in front of him. I'm not going to break down in front of him. If I start to feel emotional, I'll walk out.

Sergeant Jackson tells us to follow our daily routines to give Cedric a sense of normalcy from us. "If you wear make-up, wear it," he says. "If you do your hair, do it." So I do as he says. We get garbed up in gowns, masks, hand covers, shoe covers.

We get to his room. Sandra makes a beeline for the doctors and nurses in the room. I can't quite move just yet. I stand in the doorway. I'm slowly scanning him from the foot of the bed upward. It takes me a full two minutes to get to his bedside.

Once I am standing next to him, I see his face, and a calm comes over me.

That's my husband. I recognize him, and it's okay for me from then on. At this point, I no longer think he can die. I wasn't sure he was aware that his legs were gone, and that was difficult to consider at that moment.

They were slowly bringing him out of the coma. He was alert enough that if I called his name, he would open his eyes. His eyes would tear up when he heard my voice. Sandra and I tag-teamed praying over him and spending private time crying out of his presence.

Before I left home for this trip of a lifetime — after I'd had the revelation in the cul-de-sac in my socks — I got my wits about me and put together prayer boards with motivational sentences and scripture and family photos. When he woke up, I needed him to be surrounded by his life. I wanted him to see that he *was still Cedric, every part: his family, his military career, his achievements. I wanted him to wake up every day and see all these wonderful things in his life as reminders to get better, as reminders that this is still how we see you. I wanted him to know unconditionally: You're still the same person to us; you just don't have as much of your legs as before!*

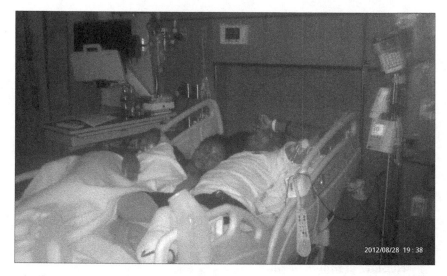

Khieda sleeps alongside me in the hospital bed.

I put the words, "I'm Still Me," in the center.

On the third day at Walter Reed, his sedation had been reduced to very little, so when he woke up that morning, he was agitated, hitting his chest, and he kept trying to tug at his breathing tube.

The doctors take the tube out of his mouth. Cedric coughs, he burps. And he starts talking. And he does not stop! His first words are to a nurse in the room.

"Come here," he says to her. When she reaches his bedside, he

tells her, "You don't take that mess from anybody. This is your OR. Don't let anybody talk down to you."

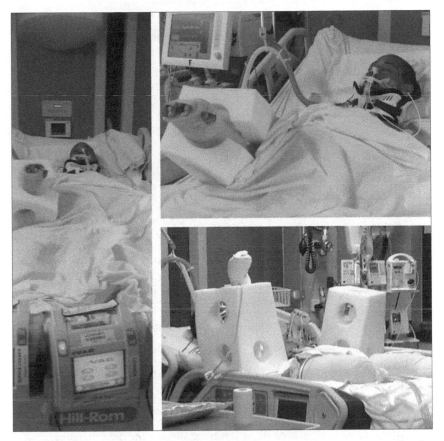

Khieda took these pictures in August of 2012 when I was still in a coma at Bethesda, seven days after I stepped on the bomb. After I woke up, she and my mother remained at my bedside.

I felt a giant, giant sense of relief: This is Cedric. Cedric's okay.

As the day goes on, we are watching the Olympics on TV. We're in and out of his room. He's in good spirits, and he knows he's in the hospital. At one point, he looks down at the foot of the bed and says, "Where's the foot?"

Sandra and I are on either side of his bed. We look at each other: he doesn't know. Sandra backs away from his bedside; she knows this is something I have to tell him.

"Babe," I say, "you're here because you stepped on an IED."

He lets out the most gut-wrenching wail that I've ever heard. It's so short. Then he cries for maybe a minute or two. Then he stops himself and asks:

"Okay, what about the other foot?"

I look at his mom, then back at him.

"This sucks, babe. They had to take that one, too, to save your life." I tell him he's going to get prosthetics.

He lets out another short cry, then says, "It's okay. I'll go on."

That's the end of his breakdown. I don't know what's going on in his mind. A little later, he's talking to people and he doesn't look like he's stressed out, but I'm thinking, it's gotta be in there.

He talks nonstop. Sandra and I don't leave that night. He seems afraid to go to sleep because he is having surgery the next morning. He's speaking in a thick, country accent — not his regular voice — but during the night, he starts to seem a little off in what he's saying. It's spooky to us; he had been talking nonstop since the morning, and now he is seriously having a conversation with the Devil.

"You think you got me?" he demands of the empty corner of the room. "I see you over there laughing at me. You don't have me! I see you lookin' at me. You tried to kill me!"

Sandra and I try to get his attention, but he never acknowledges us. Sandra screams, "He's under a Satan attack! Oh, my goodness, Satan, you walked into the wrong momma's child's room!" She starts praying out loud.

Cedric continues yelling at the empty corner: "You have no authority in here, in this room, over me! You don't have any authority in this hospital!"

I just go to his side and start waving my hands up and down his body as Sandra prays. I touch Cedric's arm, start waving my other arm up and down over his body, and begin singing the gospel song, "Because of Who You Are."

He stays fixated and talking to the Devil in the corner, but his mom and I are determined to drive it away. Eventually, Cedric stops talking to the Devil, and he starts thanking God.

After that, he keeps talking through the rest of the night and all the next day. He talks for more than 24 hours straight!

For the next week, we wait for the ball to drop. He is fragile at first, asking us not to leave him if there are strangers in the room. But he grows more comfortable. And he gets stronger super fast. He is quickly moved to his own room in the ICU.

He has so many visitors. We meet Ms. Joan, and we bond with her and thank her for her prayers upon his arrival. We Skype with the girls so they can see their dad. One day I tell them, "Put your hands on your knees. That is where Dad's legs stop now." Then we turn the camera around and show them Cedric's legs.

Khamya says, "Oh, Dad, your legs are so cute!"

Cedric has been worried about how they are going to take it. He wonders, "Are you guys still gonna love me? What does this mean? I'm not the same guy."

I tell him, "Sure, there's been a physical change, but that doesn't mean anything — I didn't marry you because of your legs. Amari and Khamya don't call you Dad because of your legs."

The weekend of his birthday, September 7th, the girls come up to Bethesda for the first time. I take them in his room, and it's empty. I know he's around here somewhere. I take them down to the cafeteria to get something to eat. When we get down there, I turn around and there's this guy just staring at us — I mean staring hard at us. He's got this little smirk like he's in heaven.

The girls see him, and they run up to him — they haven't seen him in person since he was deployed in February. They want a ride on his motorized wheelchair.

Just like that, he's taking them up and down the hallway, and it's the best thing ever.

2

The Obstacle is the Blessing

"You do not realize now what I am doing, but later you will understand."

John 13:7

THAT SCRIPTURE, JOHN 13:7, spoken by Jesus, appears on the page for July 25, 2012, in the daily devotional book that my mother prays on every morning. She read those prophetic words before she even knew that her only child was undergoing life-saving surgery more than 11,000 miles away.

Now, years after the injury, I understand exactly what this means. In fact, this message is the essence of my belief of how God works in our lives. He throws huge obstacles at us, and at first they seem like a curse, but they are actually the greatest blessing you could imagine.

Losing my legs in Afghanistan, of course, seemed like the end for me. I'll tell you more about what happened when I woke up after eight days in a coma, and learned that the boss of the battlefield had been reduced to a double amputee.

Reduced, so I thought.

What I have come to learn is that by taking away my legs and forcing me to reinvent myself, God was making me bigger and better than ever. As I've learned how to walk, run, cycle, climb mountains, swim, ski, and give motivational speeches on stages around the world, I have come to discover this:

Obstacles and blessings are twins.

With every obstacle, a blessing follows.

Science backs this up. My Army training required me to understand physics, including Newton's Third Law of Relativity. It says: "For every action, there is an equal and opposite reaction." So, when one thing presses on a second thing, the second thing simultaneously presses back in equal magnitude and opposite direction.

When I translate this into real life, it means that your blessing will be as big as your obstacle! And if you're facing a huge obstacle, like I did, then your blessings will be huge as well.

At first, when I was dealing with too many painful surgeries to count, and no confirmation from doctors that I would ever walk again, it was hard to see past the negativity.

It would have been easy to spiral down into despair. But I am a child of God, and my deep, lifelong faith wouldn't let me give up. Nor would all the prayers that my wife and family were pouring over me. And for as long as I could remember, my mother had been telling me I'd be something great someday.

So, I had to brainwash myself into believing that. I did it by flipping the way I looked at my seemingly horrible plight. I began by reading books that taught me that thoughts are things, and that our subconscious mind has more power than we can ever understand. *Think and Grow Rich* by Napoleon Hill, and *The Power of Your Subconscious*

Mind by Dr. Joseph Murphy taught me that we can reprogram ourselves to think in a new way.

That's what I did, and it saved my life. Now I'm here to teach you how to transform your thinking so you can see that with every burden comes a blessing. Here's how to begin.

PRACTICE GRATITUDE

I actually thank God for the pain that I endure every day. It forces me to feel grateful for all the blessings in my life, and the blessings that I can share with others. Every day, I feel pain in my legs because the bone continues to grow at the point where my legs were amputated. The pain is so bad, it feels like fire is burning at the points where I lost my legs. I also have phantom pain. I sometimes wake up in the middle of the night feeling a horrible sensation in my foot — a foot that is no longer there! I cannot massage the pain away because the foot does not exist!

But let me show you how I transform this pain into blessings. Once, when I was standing in the airport security line, the pain was excruciating. Rather than dwell on that, however, I put a smile on my face and started thanking God for all the good things in my life: my amazing wife, Khieda; our daughters, who are healthy and thriving in school; our beautiful home that was at the time being built as a gift from the Gary Sinise Foundation, which helps wounded warriors; the opportunity to travel and give speeches that help other people feel better and take action to improve their lives; and on and on. I continued with this dialogue in my head as people came up to me and said, "Thank you for your service." I gave zero indication to any of these people that I was suffering.

Then when I arrived at the gate, I saw someone whom I'd met at the conference where I'd just spoken. He was a reporter for *Forbes* magazine, and he asked if he could interview me for a story about Howard Schultz, then-CEO of Starbucks. This amazing opportunity was proof that God was rewarding me for persevering through the pain, and now He was blessing me in a big way! Being profiled in one of the most respected magazines in the world could lead to more speaking opportunities that benefit thousands of people.

Speak to your Obstacles!

Too often, we give our obstacles dominance over us by allowing them to beat us down with discouraging words.

"You'll never get better! It will always hurt! You'll never heal!"

"After your divorce, no one will ever love you again."

"You lost your job, now you'll be homeless and never recover."

"You'll never beat your drug addiction."

"You will never have the means to dig yourself out of this debt you've accumulated."

"You're so worthless, you deserve to be depressed. Life isn't worth living anymore."

Wrong! Wrong! Wrong!

If you were in an argument with someone and they were yelling mean things at you, you would shout back and contradict everything they were saying.

Do that in your own head.

Shout down your obstacles. Declare:

"I'm going to win! You can't beat me! I am a victor, not a victim!"

"My story is triumphant, not tragic!"

"I will walk again. Not only that, I will run the toughest race in America: the Boston Marathon!"

Be bold in your declarations of health, healing, and recovery.

Speak positive words over your obstacles, whether they're your finances, self-doubt, frustration, a relationship, fear of failure, a health crisis, or death of a loved one. Every time your obstacle tries to discourage you, snap back with a pre-made retort. Better yet, praise as if what you want is already done:

"Thank you, God, that I am healed and healthy."

"Lord, I am grateful that you restored joy to my marriage."

"God, I thank you for resolving this problem in a way that's even better than what I'd hoped for."

Get creative! Think of your obstacle as a person. Tell it off. Unleash a verbal whipping on it so it knows you're the boss, and that you will defeat it. Let your imagination run wild in how you address your burdens.

Don't be afraid of thanking your obstacles for awakening the dragon within you to see that you desire and deserve better. You can say, "Thank you, pain, for making me see just how blessed I am." Another affirmation is: "I appreciate this problem because it forced me to change my life for the better."

You know that saying, "Keep your friends close and your enemies closer"? Well, if you think of your obstacle as the enemy, keep it close, so you can stop its ability to hurt you anymore. Play mind games with it. Trick it. And just know that you have all the power to use it as a catalyst to become your greatest version.

Rethink the Obstacle as a Blessing

On many dark nights over the three years that I spent recovering from my injuries at Walter Reed, I sat alone, contemplating the tragic turn of events in my life.

"God, why did this happen to me?" I asked through pain and tears. All I wanted was to go back in time and have my legs again. "When is it going to get better?"

I never got the answers I wanted.

Until I started to ask different questions:

"How can this benefit me?"

"How can this benefit someone else?"

"How can this be a blessing?"

"What is this trying to teach me?"

"How can this be of service to me and others?"

At the same time, the words that my mother had spoken over me since childhood began to click in my mind and heart. She had said that I was going to grow up to do great things, and that God had something very special for me.

What if this was it? What if God had to cause an interruption in the circuit of my life for me to believe and become something different? That's where I was. Something was broken in the circuit. Maybe this was the very thing that Mom was talking about.

"It *has* to be this!" I decided right there in the hospital room.

No, I wasn't dealt a perfect hand, but I decided I can still win. My body was broken, but my mind, my heart, and my spirit were still the same old Cedric King. A child of God. A messenger to tell others about the power of believing and changing your life for the better.

As soon as I began to shift my thoughts, I recognized through new clarity all the amazing things that had happened since the accident.

President Barack Obama visited wounded veterans at Walter Reed Hospital once every quarter. On September 11, 2012, my family and I shared this proud moment that became the first of several visits with President Obama, including trips to the White House. Photographs courtesy Barack Obama Presidential Library.

Vice President Joe Biden and his wife, Dr. Jill Biden, invited us and the families of other military heroes for Thanksgiving Dinner at their home for several years in a row.

I gave a motivational talk to the Carolina Panthers and became friends with my hero, Cam Newton. I met Starbucks CEO Howard Schultz and Cigna CEO David Cordani. Khieda and I received a golf lesson from Vice President Joe Biden in front of his home. I'd been on many national TV shows and traveled with Montel Williams, who has become a good friend.

I was running marathons. I completed an Ironman competition. I climbed Stone Mountain in Georgia. And Khieda and I had visited the White House several times.

I had an epiphany in December of 2013, as we dined with President and Mrs. Obama, the US Deputy Secretary of Defense Ash Carter and his wife, Stephanie Carter, and other wounded veterans in the White House dining room. I was overwhelmed with gratitude and amazement about everything. Not to mention, the food was delicious beyond words, including the goat cheese appetizers, which I had never had in my life, and the dry-aged ribeye.

Being there and having this amazing experience inspired me to step back and really look at where God had brought me. Was it just good luck that all these incredible things were happening? Or were my faithfulness and positive attitude enabling God to shower us with the blessings that He promises? The story of Job came to mind; he suffered terribly and lost everything. The message was that God will cause us to lose things in life, but we will be rewarded with blessings that are twice as good. Then I remembered my mother's words. And everything started to connect.

The more I persevered through the pain with grace and gratitude, the more God blessed me and my family. Plus, I was doing what I'd always wanted to do: be a motivational speaker. Now I had my survival story, and countless anecdotes as a result, to deliver impactful messages about transforming obstacles into blessings.

I love using metaphors to share these messages; one of my favorite ways to explain how the burden is the blessing is by comparing it to baking a cake. When God turns on the proverbial heat in our lives — delivering problems and challenges that seem impossible — we usually think of the "heat" as something bad. But going through the heat is sometimes the only way to create something as sweet, delicious, and beautiful as a cake — which is usually presented and savored during celebrations.

So when it comes to baking a cake, the heat is a positive force. The cake cannot exist without it. At room temperature, it's just a soupy mess in the pan. You can't eat it. In fact, some of the raw ingredients might even make you sick if you ingest them. The cake is created in a very hot oven. If you leave it in the heat long enough, it cooks into something delightful.

My point is, don't be afraid to take the heat of life. Know that it's "baking" you into something better, and can even take you to your Making Point.

Oh, wait, I have another favorite example: World Heavyweight Champion Muhammad Ali. If he had not lost to Joe Frazier, he would never have beaten the reputedly unbeatable George Foreman. In fact, he would have probably gotten killed.

But the Fraser defeat taught Muhammad Ali what it feels like to be low. That experience, when his boxing license was revoked, propelled him. It taught him how to use the enemy against itself, and it honed his warrior spirit. That enabled him to defeat George Foreman by making his opponent use his own strength against himself.

Think of your obstacle as life providing you with a sparring partner. The sparring partner is not trying to hurt you; it's trying to help you get better. Look at it in a new way, and you will become a fighter, a winner, no matter who or what your opponent might be. You might get punched or even knocked down. But when you persevere through the pain, you will be rewarded with blessings beyond belief.

How To Transform Your Obstacles into Blessings

Here are some questions for you to define your obstacles and explore how you can flip the script on your thinking and transform your burdens into blessings.

What is the biggest obstacle you've had to face in life?

_____

_____

_____

_____

How can this be a blessing?

_____

_____

_____

_____

What is your resistance?

_____

_____

_____

_____

How can this pain be your teacher?

_____

_____

_____

_____

How can you look at this obstacle as your greatest life lesson to become your best?

_____

_____

_____

_____

Make a list of how this obstacle has changed you.

_____

_____

_____

_____

Now list the benefits that resulted from those changes.

_____

_____

_____

_____

How can you draw strength from the mental and physical pain to improve your life?

_____

_____

_____

_____

Explore how your faith provides the foundation for your ability to triumph over difficulties.

_____

_____

_____

_____

What would it take for you to see this obstacle as a gift?

_____

_____

_____

_____

3

Flexing Your
Find-Your-Feet Muscle

As an Army Ranger, I was known for running everywhere.

Not walking.

Running.

I would even run to the gym to work out. I routinely led hundreds of soldiers on five-mile runs at the crack of dawn. And if we had an Army competition, you better believe I was among the first to reach the finish line.

So, losing my legs, and having to choose new ways to get around, has been a difficult challenge. The warrior in me wants to start everything new at 100 miles an hour; my double-amputee reality requires me to begin at one mile per hour.

No, make that zero.

Because everything is new.

And everything has a learning curve.

Plus, I don't like taking the easy way out. Comfort feels too easy. I want a challenge.

"You're never going to get me back in that chair," I declared to the prosthetist Mike Corcoran, my physical therapist, and Khieda as I rose out of a wheelchair and stepped into my prosthetic legs to learn how to walk.

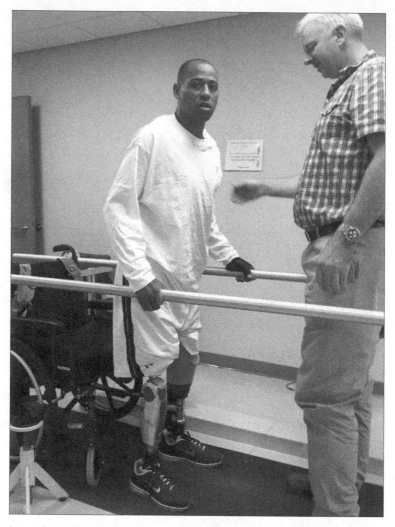

I took my first steps on my new prosthetic legs in the Military Advanced Training Center (MATC) at Walter Reed, during the first week of November 2012, just over three months after the explosion. My amazing prosthetist, Mike Corcoran, tailor-made these and about 30 more pairs for me since then.

I have stayed true to that declaration; six years after my injury, I sit in a wheelchair only as a last resort. The same goes for motorized scooters. I have every reason in the world to use them. And nobody would bat an eye if I did.

But that's not me.

Especially not since I activated my find-your-feet muscle. You've never heard of this because it's not taught in anatomy class. It's not even a muscle.

It's a way of thinking.

I came up with the idea for a find-your-feet muscle during grueling, painful moments, coping with the fact that *I have no feet*. I wanted to walk, run, drive, ride a bike, swim, and do anything and everything I used to do with feet.

And do it all even better.

Nothing was going to stop me.

So I had to compensate for my lack of feet by fueling my brain with such overwhelming faith in myself, it's like I created a whole new muscle in my body.

My find-your-feet muscle.

It's a power within yourself that you can only unlock with your thoughts.

It allows you to excel *without* the thing you lost, that you thought you could only do *with* that particular *thing*.

On the surface, this sounds crazy. But I was desperate to regain my freedom, my independence, and my self-reliance. Losing my mobility and depending on doctors, nurses, physical therapists, and my wife to do everything was extremely difficult. I'm a soldier. A survivor. Someone who knows how to persevere through the toughest conditions — battle zones, swamps, frigid temperatures, mountainsides — and come out alive and unscathed.

So it didn't surprise me that after the injury, my fighting spirit became even stronger. In fact, from the day I woke up from the coma, I was talking about driving again, and I became obsessed with learning how to drive, even though I had yet to receive my prosthetic legs and master walking on them.

Driving symbolized freedom and power over my life, as well as moving fast and getting where I wanted to go. That was the opposite of when I felt stuck in my hospital bed.

So, as soon as I could, I got into my power chair and rolled to the office of Captain Tammy Phipps, my occupational therapist and driver's ed teacher who ran the Driving Rehabilitation Program at Walter Reed.

"When can I drive?" I asked. "What do I have to do to drive?"

Captain Phipps was amused by my enthusiasm. The conversation about driving generally happens early on, but the actual timeframe for getting behind the wheel — though it varies dramatically from person to person — is about a month or two after a person goes from inpatient to outpatient. And that was a very long way off for me.

"First, Cedric, you've got pins in your hands," Captain Phipps said. "And you haven't been medically cleared to drive."

I started asking my doctors, my physical therapist, and anybody who had anything to do with getting me cleared to drive. I called nonprofits who supported amputees by donating modified vehicles, who'd then turn around and call Captain Phipps and ask her when I could drive. It got to the point where she'd answer her phone and know it was somebody calling on my behalf to ask, "What does Sergeant King need to do to start driving?"

At the same time that I was asking, "What do I have to do to drive?" I was also saying, "If you're going to tell me no, you better be able to tell me why, so I can know what benchmark I need to hit."

Finally, my orthopedic doctor made an exception and gave me early release to learn how to drive because I had 20 years of driving experience — and I believed in my heart that I could do it.

"You'll be learning to drive with your hands," the doctors told me, "in a specially modified car provided by Walter Reed."

"Whatever I need to do," I told them. "I'm ready."

I couldn't get behind the wheel fast enough!

But when the moment finally comes, and I'm sitting in the driver's seat of a car designed to teach amputees how to drive with our hands, I'm a nervous wreck.

Fortunately, Captain Phipps puts me at ease in the modified Chevy.

"The trick is getting comfortable," she says. "This is driving, but it's driving in a different way. You have to trust the equipment. You have to relax."

I am downright giddy. Here I am, an infantry soldier, a warrior, and I feel like a 14-year-old getting to drive for the first time on the family farm.

I want to conquer this hand-driving experience in a blink, and speed away on the busy streets of Bethesda, as if I've been driving here all my life. My eagerness prevents me from considering that I grew up in a small town in the South, and I have no big-city driving experience.

Herein lies another lesson. When we start new things, we want to master them in a heartbeat. We want mastery to come easily and quickly. We want to rush to the accomplishment. Sitting there in a hand-operated vehicle, I realize that I have to start where I am: at one. I can work my way up to 10. But if I think I can hop into the car and start at 10, I am cheating the experience. This mindset applies to any experience, not just learning to drive after your legs are amputated.

So, I start by learning how to adjust the seat and the mirrors. The floor-mounted stick works like the throttle/brake on a boat: push in to give the car gas, pull back to brake. The steering wheel has a spinner, which I use to steer with my left hand.

Captain Phipps' passenger floor has a brake, but other than that function, I'm doing all the driving. I'm the one controlling the vehicle.

"It's not just driving," she says. "It's your ability to get your roles back in life. You get to take your wife on a date. You get to drive your daughters around. This first time out is a faith walk."

She's right. As I pull into traffic and start driving, I can't stop the automatic response of wanting to move my legs to engage the gas and brake pedals. It's like my body is stuck in years of driving memory. So, I really have to concentrate on using my arms. I've got to respect the process of allowing my body to get in sync with what my brain is telling it to do: drive with my hands, not my feet.

After my first drive, we pull back onto base, and the guard asks for my ID. I hand it over to him. He examines it, looks at me, and hands my ID back. "All right," he says. "Have a good day."

Captain Phipps asks, "How did that feel?"

I glance at her. "Normal! It felt normal!" I want to shout, *I'm so excited!* I just drove for the first time with no legs! Cars honked at me, swerved, passed me, yielded the right of way to me, treated me like I was a regular old driver on the road. To top it off, this mundane, boring interchange between the guard and myself has made this the most equalizing day since July 25, 2012. This is an awesome moment! This moment is a gift!

I want to keep pushing it, so the next time we drive, Captain

Phipps has me drive into DuPont Circle, where half a dozen streets merge into one giant roundabout. These roundabouts are all over the Washington, DC area. And I'm totally confused!

"Tammy, what are the rules here? How do I navigate around this thing?"

She gives me some pointers, and somehow I make it. I'm feeling good about it.

Our next hurdle is getting on the Capital Beltway. When the time comes, my heart hammers in my chest. *What? I just conquered the city streets. Now you want me to get on that 64-mile freeway loop around DC that's 12 lanes wide in some places?* Not to mention that the Beltway is notorious for bottlenecks.

So I tell myself, *Cedric, it's time to engage your find-your-feet muscle. I'm not using it. Fear is paralyzing it. Time to flex!*

"Yeah, I can do this," I announce, heading down a freeway entrance ramp.

You cannot play games on the on-ramp. You have to anticipate where to put your car to merge onto the busy freeway. You've got to be aggressive. Look over your shoulder. Even when you're driving with legs, you've got to be on your game on the Beltway. So here I am, learning how to drive with my hands in the most frightening traffic of my life. The noise of fear is blaring in my mind. It's painful. Scary.

You can't do this. You're going to crash! You won't make it...

Negative thoughts cloud my concentration. In the middle of this wild traffic I have to force myself to push past my chaotic thoughts. I had done this exact mental exercise so many times during the toughest times during Ranger School, while crossing frigid swamps in the dark, going without food and sleep, and surviving dangerous drills. So I smash the fear, panic, and pessimistic thinking, by thanking God for blessing me with the power to master driving with my hands on the Beltway.

That creates instant calm in my mind, and I'm finally able to focus on the present, one blinker light and lane change at a time. I am so grateful as Captain Phipps and I return to Walter Reed. I conquered my demons by flexing my find-your-feet muscle, which really meant drawing on God's power to do what I was unable to do for myself in those moments of fear, worry, and doubt.

After beating the Beltway, my next driving goal is to take Khieda on a date in DC, so Captain Phipps and I conduct reconnaissance. I choose the restaurant, and Captain Phipps drives the route so I will know how to drive Khieda and myself there when the time comes.

By the time I take Khieda out for a date, I'm respecting the process and allowing my body to synchronize with my brain. No more phantom legs or feet trying to push pedals. It's all about the mind and the hands now. I'm still as giddy as a 14-year-old, and the idea of taking my wife on a date makes me feel like a new man.

As my driving skills improve, my confidence surges. After five driving sessions with Captain Phipps, it's time for Khieda to join us. I'm so excited to finally give Khieda a break from driving me everywhere. I'm looking forward to driving *her* around with ease and confidence through this big-city traffic.

Khieda is nervous, but she knows how much I want to be independent. She knows I'll learn to drive well — no matter what it takes. By now, I've got a pretty good handle on the new system, pulling forward to brake, pushing inward to accelerate.

Though I'm always grateful to have the wheelchair loaded into the car and unloaded by someone else, because that keeps me mobile, driving is freedom. It represents a new life. I don't have to depend on and wear out Khieda. She is my backbone, and she needs a break. If I can give her a chance to rest and take care of herself while I drive myself around, that is a gift I can give her in exchange for the miracles that she has given to me since I woke up from the coma.

Learning how to drive with Captain Phipps was an experience I will always cherish. We had so much fun together, telling stories and laughing. We'd been brought together in this very morbid situation, and yet we are bonding over this simple, very normal act of driving a car. She is part of my journey back to success.

Working through this process with her illustrates a success formula that I created: *Belief + Effort = Gets You Where You Want.*

FLASH BACK TO A FATEFUL MOMENT; FLASH FORWARD TO THE FUTURE

Learning to drive without legs is strengthening my find-your-feet muscle. The exhilaration of conquering such an intimidating feat gives me courage to do bigger and better things. That's how I felt in the Army, so I'm starting to feel like myself again. Then I realize:

I'm still me.

When I woke up from the coma, I didn't know if I would ever be able to say that. At that moment, I didn't know if I'd ever feel like the original Cedric.

In fact, when I first wake up, I think I'm in an operating room, because nurses and doctors are tending to me and there are endless monitors around the bed. Plus, the tube down my throat that prevents me from talking is just one of many tubes attached to my body. My right arm is propped up in this orange triangular foam cushion that looks like a giant cheese wedge. My vision is a little blurry, but I'm certain that my wife and my mom are standing beside the bed.

What are you guys doing here? Am I in Afghanistan? Is this a dream?
Then I learn the five W's of my new reality.

Who: Army Ranger turned Wounded Warrior and Double Amputee.

What: A long and uncertain road to recovery ahead.

When: Now.

Where: This word begins the most horrifying questions of my life: *Where's the foot? Where are the legs?*

Why: Khieda tells me the brutal truth, that my legs were amputated to save my life. And I instantly feel as low as I can ever remember being in my life.

My soul is just *done*. That's a bad day. A tough, tough, TOUGH, moment.

I cry hard. Really hard. But grief triggers my find-your-feet muscle.

"Okay, we're gonna get through this," I declare from my heart.

Maybe all my survival training wrenched me up from complete devastation in that moment and gave me the strength to say, "Okay." Actually, there's no way I could have created a high-quality thought so quickly in my mind. It was pure God, sending a jolt of resilience through me, activating the residual power of a lifetime of prayers.

My legs feel numb.

But they're gone.

They had to take your legs because they were losing you. The only way to save you was to amputate. It was either them amputate or you dying.

What if I had been conscious, and the doctors had asked, *Master Sergeant King, would you like us to amputate your legs to save your life?*

Of course, I would have chosen life over legs.

The shock is having that decision made for you. I confess, I had thought about being shot or blown to bits, dying right there on the battlefield. I had contemplated the risk of being taken hostage and being killed. But never in a thousand guesses would I have considered the possibility of this — lying in Walter Reed with no legs.

When I finally focus across the hospital room, I am awed by the vision boards and prayer boards that Khieda has created and posted on the walls. We have always used vision boards in our lives to display our dreams for the world to see.

Please, create your dream board! Take a poster board, and cover it with pictures, words, drawings — anything that displays what you want. Write words like "peace" and "health," and paste photos of your dream home or an outfit that you'll wear after you lose weight. If you want to take a dream vacation to Fiji, get brochures and cut out pictures of the resort where you'll stay, and the beach where you'll swim. If you want to get married, but have not met your ideal partner, post inspiring quotes about love, images of weddings, and pictures of happy couples.

Dream boards and prayer boards force you to have a clear picture. They help you visualize the outcome that you want to occur, even if it seems impossible at the moment. When you wake up in the morning, you can say, *Let me think of the outcome I want to occur today. Let me do the work of putting my mind toward that outcome, even if I'm not physically there.*

Say to yourself, *Listen, I got this. I will believe in the impossible every time. By believing in what I can't see, it will inevitably visualize and materialize.* Say this out loud. Believe it.

In 2007, long before I lost my legs, I changed the screensaver on my computer to a picture of a white BMW 7 Series. Every day from 2007 until 2011, I looked at the car of my dreams when I was on my computer. Though I was driving an 18-year-old Nissan at the time, I believed in my heart that someday, somehow, I would get my dream car.

Finally, after five years of looking at my dream car on my screensaver, I became the proud owner of my white BMW 7 Series in December of 2012, thanks to a grant that my driving instructor helped me secure. At the time, I still had to pass the driving test, which I did in April of 2013. Then I was free to drive my dream car!

I believe that looking at an image of what I wanted helped me materialize the dream into fruition. It really works! Try it, please.

Likewise, photos are powerful reminders of our blessings. For example, as I'm lying in the hospital bed, my buddies send pictures to encourage me. One Ranger instructor shared a photo of students walking through swamps, submerged in cold water during the winter. I know all too well from my days as a student in Ranger School how painful that is.

Their support makes me smile. And the pictures inspire a surprising thought: *I may be in the hospital with no legs, but at least I'm not tired, cold, and miserable in hypothermia-inducing cold water in the middle of the night!*

I know in my heart that I've endured tougher, more painful situations. And I keep thinking, *This soft, warm hospital bed is way better than that swamp! Things can always be worse — and I've known worse!*

Again, a simple attitude change helped me flex my find-your-feet muscle. Flipping the switch from negative to positive is not always fast or easy. But I do it every time. If I don't, seeds of doubt sprout in my mind. They grow into unruly fears that can shoot roots down into a deep, dark depression.

My family is constantly at my side, especially Khieda, and my friends and relatives come from great distances to hug me and bring me joy. But sometimes during the night, when it's quiet and still, my mind churns over a repetitive checklist of thoughts:

1. I don't have legs; how could this be good?

2. Without legs, here's something that is good: I do have the love of my wife and daughters.

3. I do get a chance to talk to people when I'm not in surgery; I can call my mom and family and talk.

4. I have time to reflect and think about my next move.

5. I have an opportunity to inspire people around me.

This checklist inspires an epiphany about the power of a smile. It's so simple, but I know people are motivated by a smile. That's why I naturally smile at everybody, even when I'm in pain. *Especially* when I'm in pain. I ask people to come into my room and their spirits uplift me, while mine uplifts them. It creates an endless cycle of giving and receiving little bursts of happiness. It gives me hope. I realize that if I smile and carry on with my life, I am giving others a blessing. It feels like the craziest thought. It's like not understanding electricity, but knowing that when I plug in the lamp, it works.

About two weeks after my injury, United States Deputy Secretary of Defense Ash Carter and his wife Stephanie Carter visit me as part of their regular weekend stops at Walter Reed to talk with wounded soldiers.

I'm honored to meet them, and I tell them about my desire to spread positivity to others. I also share my athletic goals — to run a 5K. I wear a brave face, but I realize it's just my face. It's who I am.

Not all moments in those early days are so brave. Sometimes I try to bargain with God: *I wish it were just one leg.* I quickly remember and realize that bargaining with God is not an option. Nor is trying to figure out the answer to the question: *Why me?*

I want to tell you about the low places my mind has gone as I've tried to find peace and purpose in this tragedy that I turn into a triumph every single day. Many nights I would lie in my hospital bed, fully awake, just aching with hopelessness. A horrible anguish would overtake my entire body and mind as I felt robbed of my identity.

I am a combat infantryman. I am not only at the top of my field, but I am combat tested — twice. I am a graduate of elite institutes. I am an Airborne Ranger. I am a US Army Jumpmaster. I can deploy troops on land and in air. I am in the top one percent. I am at the top of my skill set. I am practiced and proficient in my profession on the battlefield.

I am in great shape. I can go to any unit anywhere in the Army and prove myself to be one of the top guys, if not the top guy altogether. I am a competitor. I can try to outrun or out-push any of my peers. I am respected by all the soldiers who've ever served under me and those superiors I've served under. I am feared by young soldiers because they don't know what kind of workout I will give them. I am proud of all of my reports and evaluations.

I have overcome every piece of adversity I've ever faced on the job. In combat, I have always departed and succeeded in every situation. I have badges on my uniform.

I am proud of my accomplishments.

After all these years in the Army, I am finally and exactly the person I always wanted to be. If I were an 18-year-old kid looking up to somebody, I would want that person to be me.

And now here I am.

And you're telling me I'm not that person anymore?

Oh, wait, I'm not a Sergeant anymore?

What good is living if I can't be Sergeant King? If I can't be myself?

Man, this sucks.

All that I am — or I think that I am — is gone.

In those moments, in that low, low place where I'm questioning who I am, I wonder, *What's the point of waking me up from this coma if I can't be the person I want to be?*

I know I have to find another way, which can only come from inside me. So I plead with God:

Help me find another way to hurry up and start living a different way, or go ahead and kill me now!

As I continued to lie there, wallowing in my pity party, I saw no way to move upward and forward. Nor could I go backwards in time to July 24, 2012, and re-play the next day with a different outcome.

My only option is to hurry up and get to living again. Yes, hurry up and get to living again. Easier said than done.

I have to take action. I have to stop looking down at my new, different self, and start looking outside of myself.

So, I look up at the wall of my room at the Wall of Love, wall-papered with prayer boards and vision boards, filled with pictures of my wife, my daughters, my mom, my aunts, uncles, cousins, my grandparents, my friends, my soldiers, my superiors, and posters, hats, flowers, cards. All the moments captured in those pictures were preparing me, us, for this challenge. Those images and the love and protection they cast over me are my armor. My spirit is fortified by the words that Khieda wrote at the center of one vision board:

I'm Still Me.

Khieda knew this best of all, even amid her anguish after that initial phone call and throughout the subsequent updates that yet another amputation had occurred to save my life. Though it had still been unknown when I would be home, she followed a Providential drive to create these prayer-vision boards for my room for when I eventually arrived at Walter Reed.

She'd felt our spirits connect when I was still in Afghanistan, still in a coma, still fighting for my life, and she heard my voice say, "I'm still me." She knew the vision boards would remind me of who I was, *who I am,* and that they would serve the same purpose in our lives as always: to show what we want, before we know how we're going to get it.

I thank God every day for blessing me with my wife, Khieda Jackson, who epitomizes unconditional love and truly lives our vow "in sickness and in health."

So, in addition to visuals, she put statements affirming that: *I Am Alive. I Am Blessed. I Am Loved. I'm Still God's Child. I'm Still Here. I'm Still Able.*

I'm Still Me.

Khieda. My wife, Khieda, the love of my life.

Looking at that wall, studying the messages, and remembering the times when the photographs were taken, I gradually rise up from middle-of-the-night despair into peaceful relief that yes, I am still me, and I'm giving thanks to Khieda for being by my side.

LIFE'S GREATEST BLESSING SO FAR: MY WIFE, KHIEDA

As for how we met, I did not just snap my fingers and Khieda magically appeared. Like everything else, I had to start at one. I improvised and won her over. Well, not exactly. It started when I ventured from North Carolina all the way to Fort Lewis in Tacoma, Washington, almost 3,000 miles from home. In the Pacific Northwest, I am no longer in the South near my friends: Kenya, Kelly, or my sister-cousin Jennifer. My first adult relationship has just ended, and I am determined that if I find love again, I would work to keep it. I also know that love is not just going to knock on my door, unannounced. I am not going to get to 10, aka love, without starting at one.

So, I brainstorm where pretty girls might be, and decide the most strategic starting point for my search is inside the mall on a bench directly in front of a Victoria's Secret store.

I don't care about looking stupid. It's early in my Army career, and I'm on a mission. A lot of my friends wouldn't approach a pretty girl because there's an invisible force field around them. The force field is the intimidation factor; an attractive woman gets a lot of attention, so you have to step to her with your A-game or you will strike out immediately. Suddenly, a pretty woman catches my eye, so I go in the store, introduce myself, and try to have a conversation with her while she's working. Again, I don't care if I look stupid. At the very least, I'm going to try.

She flashes this "I'm taken" ring on her finger. I leave the store, temporarily dejected, but not defeated. As I sit on the bench waiting for my buddies, I watch her in the store for a little longer.

Providence brings us together again, a short time after the ring-flashing incident. This time, she's in the convenience store at the gas station, where she's getting some ice cream. My heart propels me to talk to her, so I glance at the ice cream and say, "Oh, you don't want to get that; it'll ruin your figure."

She doesn't remember me, so I re-introduce myself. Apparently, my comment does not win her over. Nor does she give me her number. I leave the store, sit on the curb, and watch her.

Man, what do I need to say or do to get this beautiful woman to talk to me?

What I know in this moment is that she's worth talking to. My heart tells me this. Not my head, but my heart. My head is saying: *Ring-flashing means she's spoken for; not recalling my name or remembering that we'd met before means I didn't make a good impression — or any impression for that matter.*

My head is saying I just blew yet another opportunity to get her number by putting my foot in my mouth. My head is saying: *Stop embarrassing yourself.*

My heart knows looking stupid on the path from one to 10 is worth it. Always.

So, when I see her a little while later in a store in the mall, I disregard my head. My heart tells me to introduce myself again. This time, recognition lights up her face.

"Oh, Cedric," she says.

"I tried to talk to you before," I tell her. "I thought you were married." (She wasn't.)

When people say the third time's a charm, it's the truth on so many levels. It's the heart, not the head, that drives people to that third, charming time!

Khieda Jackson finally gave me her phone number.

Had I not been willing to look stupid and trust that I didn't look like a stalker by sitting outside her store and staring at her while she worked; had I given up after one try, figuring she's taken; had I given up after stumbling the second time I saw her by potentially implying that I was saying something negative about her figure (I wasn't!); had it not been for any of these factors, we may have never come together.

My head had plenty of reasons to make me stop. So many external and internal obstacles were saying no. I could have been embarrassed that third time I saw her; I could have hidden in the cough syrup aisle. I could have said to myself:

There's that beautiful woman who won't give me the time of day.
Let me stay safe and not try to talk to her again. Let me not
look stupid.

The obstacle: my brief history of rejection with this woman.

The blessing: God kept putting us in the same place at the same time. I could not ignore that. That was the beginning of our beautiful relationship. I didn't know just how deep it would go, but at the time, I was a very happy man!

Fast forward all these years, and here I am in Walter Reed with my beautiful wife lifting my spirits every day, even during my middle-of-the-night moments of self-doubt. She's there for me, and I need to be there for her — and me. I need to do everything possible to restore Cedric back to wholeness, for myself, for my wife, and for our daughters. I need to walk. And run.

In fact, I literally came out of the coma thinking about running, even though I was unaware that my legs were gone. As I was coming out of sedation, I try to talk, but the breathing tube won't allow it.

So my mom and Khieda give me some paper. With my bandaged hand that's missing part of a finger, I write a crinkly, scribbly "V." Khieda and my mom can't figure out what I'm trying to write so I write a jagged "A."

My dad's name was Van. "Is it Van?" they ask. I shake my head.

My step-dad's name is Valton. "Is it Valton?" they ask. I shake my head. I scribble a "D."

"Vydashon?" They say my cousin's name, even though she goes by Telese and I'm spelling her name wrong. Nobody knows why I'm calling her by her given name!

I nod, proceeding to scribble that before my deployment, Vydashon — a personal trainer — and I had vowed to run a 5K when I got back home. We are all amazed that I have just awakened from a coma and my first thought is about a running commitment with my cousin.

Then, of course, I learn that I no longer have legs. So, first I have to learn to walk again. I start talking with the doctors about walking and running.

The facts are telling me: *you're in a hospital bed; you have no legs; you're incapacitated; you can't walk; you can't run.* These facts are real. They are quantifiable. I can see these facts as plain as day.

Yet my heart isn't having anything to do with the facts. The heart knows more than the head; I know this with certainty. The heart is smarter than the head. And my heart tells me that I will run again.

God Shows Me What I Can Do: Through the Olympics

The background noise of these first days in Walter Reed is the 2012 Summer Olympics in London, which aired from July 27 to August 12.

Sitting in my hospital bed with little to do, I watch the men's 400-meter dash. There on my TV screen is a double amputee charging full speed ahead on prosthetic blades. This is not the Paralympic Games; this is South African runner Oscar Pistorius speeding around the track, competing with able-bodied runners. Hope surges through me as I stare at him in awe.

> *Man, if he can compete against able-bodied people, surely there's*
> *an opportunity for me, too.*

The doctor enters my room. I'm excited, and I start talking about running. The doc tries to be positive, but he's looking at me with an expression that says *you're not a runner*. He's right; I can't even walk. He won't stretch his imagination to say, *Yes, you can do what Oscar Pistorius is doing.*

During these same moments that the doc is trying to find an optimistic way to tell me *No*, Oscar keeps running around the track, his left shoulder displaying a tattoo of a quote from the book of Corinthians 9:26-27: "I do not run like a man who is running aimlessly."

My heart is leaping! I want other people, the doc included, to share in my excitement.

"Do you think I'll be able to run by next year?" I ask.

The doc does not look cheerful as he says, "I don't think you're going to be able to do that by next year. That may be too high a goal. Maybe re-set your goal and think realistically."

My heart breaks — for about a second.

I quickly process the feedback. *Too high a goal.* Those words from the doc register on my thoughts like the starter pistol in a race. *Pow!* My mind is off and running while the competitor in me rages: I want to compete against — and be victorious over — the doc's prognosis. I want to compete against the words, the idea, the output from someone else: "YOU WON'T BE ABLE TO." Those words found a little spot on my shoulder and sat there like a chip.

"You're saying I won't be running by next year?" I ask again.

"Yeah, nobody could do that by next year," he says.

"You mean to tell me you think I can't be running?"

"It's going to take a lot longer than you think," he says.

Nothing against the doc. He only said he didn't think I could do it because that's all he knew to say. Fortunately for me, I am a competitive Army Ranger with 20 years of military training; I prove people wrong time and again.

I'm going to be running 10 miles next year. This becomes my mantra, but as with everything, I have to start at one. At this point, with legs amputated at the knees, and with no feet, I'm nowhere close to getting prosthetics, let alone running blades. Yet I start playing the recording of my goal in my head over and over and over again: *I'm going to be running 10 miles next year.*

In the early days at Walter Reed, I realize the conversations with doctors focus on a timeframe of the next 24 hours, the next day, and the day after that. Nothing is long-term. On the positive side, that keeps me in a rhythm, but it doesn't nurture what I'm feeling on the inside.

Your heart can tell you something that's five, 10 years away. The quandary is that the head says, *THIS IS WHAT I WANT,* while your heart is saying, *I'm telling you what's going to happen in the future.*

My inner conflict is multifold: my present reality and my head are battling my long-term dreams and my heart.

Give me an indication of the long-term. I want to focus on the exciting details of my future.

My head is telling me: *You're in a place where your future doesn't count! You're in an emergency room, in an emergency situation, and all that matters is what's in front of you, right now!*

For seconds, it feels as if my heart is lying to me — telling me something so different from the reality that I have right now. I want you to know: doubters are out there! They are doubting themselves from the perspective of *if they were in your situation.* Nobody knows whether you can accomplish something except you. I realized quickly that when you ask someone if they think you can do something, what they are saying back to you is whether they think they can or can't in their conception of your circumstances, not theirs. It's like they're saying:

If I were you, I couldn't run next year.

Before losing my legs, I thought life was a story of *You Get What Life Gives You.* I now know it's the opposite. True living is about *What You Do With What Happens To You.*

If I had been so caught up on THIS IS WHAT HAPPENED, I would have totally missed Oscar running around the track. I would have only felt the heartbreak of the doctor's words. As Oscar was running, as the doc was saying no, as my heart was saying YES, I had this feeling of: *Pay attention to this moment. Be very aware of this moment. You cannot sit here and bypass this moment.*

My heart shouts: *This is a moment you must respect!*

I feel it in my heart, and I believe it's real.

What you believe is real. My situation may have looked impossible to the average person because it sure looked impossible to the doctor treating me. If I had told Oscar Pistorius what was in my heart, I imagine that he would have believed it as much as I did. If I had asked him if he thought I could run next year, I believe he'd say, "Yes."

This was a pinnacle moment of my life. I could have easily dismissed it as a coincidence and interpreted the sight of a double amputee running on TV as the doctor told me no, as a bad omen of what I could never do.

I chose to interpret that moment through the eyes of faith.

"I can do all things through Christ, who strengthens me," reads Philippians 4:13.

Having this mindset requires being sensitive to the moment you're in. Some moments are so powerful, you have to feel them, study them, apply them to do something big. But if you're not careful, those powerful moments will pass by and be gone. Wasted. Worthless.

I may have had an advantage in that moment. My life was void of the usual distractions that consume us: the job, relationships, the kids, family issues, emails, and so on. I was in a hospital bed. All the distractions and noise had been removed, so it was easy to listen to the hope in my heart, as opposed to the doctor's dismal prognosis.

I was lucky, and I want you to learn from my experience. In order to make the best decisions for yourself, the kind that you make silently in your heart and your mind and set your life on a course that others will say is crazy, requires getting quiet.

We live in such a noisy world. Phones are constantly dinging, chiming, streaming, interrupting. We are addicted to distraction. We can hardly finish one thought or conversation before a text message or alert pops up and sucks our thoughts into a tsunami of trending topics that do nothing but entertain us for a moment, an hour, a day. All this external stimulation robs us of time to go within, think, and listen. We're always moving, succumbing to the popularity of being "busy."

We trust others' opinions — especially those in authority positions such as doctors — more than what our own hearts are telling us.

But you won't find your Making Point in words or alleged wisdom flowing from someone else's mouth, or lighting up the screen on your devices, or being declared by a doctor, lawyer, banker, or professor.

Your Making Point is in your heart, and it's activated by something that feels like heartbreak. But the only way to hear it and feel it is to sit down, be quiet, and retreat to that place deep within where you can hear your heart and your intuition. This is where your spirit talks to you!

When the doctor told me no, my spirit was shouting, *Run, Cedric, run!*

I want you to really hear your own spirit giving you guidance that defies reality. This will give you a new clarity and optimism, even in the worst situation. You will just know that a better outcome will soon be your reality. No matter what your ears are hearing.

Prayer, meditation, journaling, exercise, and a healthy diet, can all help you cultivate the ability to hear your inner voice speaking to you. Some people call it mindfulness or being present in the moment. Because that's where all the action is.

Right here, right now.

Not in the past, where I got my legs blown off. Not in the future, where doctors are saying I will not run.

No, this moment right here, where I'm taking control of my thoughts, is all that matters. Circumstances have thrown me into a boxing ring with the Goliath of double amputation, and all bets are pointing to the beast beating me down for the count. But I am fighting. I am delivering a deadly blow to that dude, right in his single eye that's seeing me all wrong. And I'm slamming him down on the mat for a TKO, so I can literally stand on top of him, throw my firsts up in the air like a champ, and know that I won the world heavyweight championship of transforming my breaking point into my Making Point.

So your power to slay the beasts that are trying to beat you down lies in the moment. A split-second. We think these are infinite. But they're not. We only get so many moments in a day. Make every one of them matter!

THIS WAS ONE OF THOSE MOMENTS.

Time will keep ticking by, but you need to take a screenshot of your life during that moment, and save it to the photos in your mind's eye. You can type some text over it that says, "My Making Point" along with your goal: "I'm going to be running 10 miles next year." My screenshot was me in the hospital bed with no legs, watching a double amputee run in the Olympics, my spirit leaping to get up and run, while doc is saying no, and my heart is saying YES!

So I took another screenshot from my imagination, of myself running for miles and miles and miles on blades just like the ones that were pinging against the track as Oscar Pistorius raced at superhuman speed alongside men with two legs. I placed this second image in my mind beside the first image. And that became my goal. It's like the pictures became superimposed over the physical reality that I was seeing in the physical world with my eyes. But I knew that the power of visualization — or focusing on what you want in your imagination until it manifests in reality — really works.

So, add some courage and imagination to your formula for transforming your breaking point into your Making Point.

Activate your find-your-feet muscle by drawing on strength to move forward with something that doesn't physically exist. I don't have feet, but I'm ready to RUN! This type of thinking will reprogram our brains, and re-train our automatic responses to difficulties and harsh circumstances.

On the other hand, if you believe in the power of the obstacle, you'll lose. The obstacle will win. **You must believe in the thing that you cannot see.**

"Now faith is the substance of things hoped for, the evidence of things not seen," according to Hebrews 11:1 in the Bible.

My new mantra — *I'm going to be running 10 miles next year* — inspires me just weeks after losing my legs to start having conversations about getting prosthetics. I may be riding in a wheelchair, but I want to run. I'm constantly trying to beat down doubts about whether I would succeed at standing, walking, or running. So I draw on all the mental toughness I had cultivated in the Army to bodyslam those thoughts of defeat, and flip them to what I feel in my heart. It's literally the only thing that keeps me going.

Here's your takeaway: **sometimes all you have is what's in your heart.** That's the secret key to your Making Point. Without it, you are surrendering to your breaking point.

After a few months, I get DEXA scans so I can start working with a prosthetist. I'm super excited, thinking I'm on my way to walking and running.

"We can't let you go on prosthetics yet," they tell me. Turns out, my bones are not dense enough.

They say, "You haven't used your bones for body weight in two, three months. You have to strengthen your bones. We can re-test in two or three weeks."

Delay. Disappointment. Obstacles.

What can I do in this situation? I can follow their instructions while continuing to believe what's in my heart. And I can do everything in my power to accelerate the process. I eat every bone-strengthening food I can get on a plate in front of me.

When I have my second DEXA scan, my bones fail — again. This is disheartening, but it's not the first time I've failed at something twice. I bombed the first two times I tried to talk to Khieda, and look what happened the third time. Two failed bone density tests are not going to stop what's in my heart. If I just keep trying — eating more spinach than Popeye — I know I can succeed.

My heart drives me. All the months leading up to this, I am believing that my heart wasn't lying to me. I feel there's no way that God would be so cruel as to put something in front of me that I can't accomplish. I would never put a toy in front of my daughters and prohibit them from playing with it.

So, I continue on my bone-boosting diet. I take vitamins. I focus my mind's eye on the two screenshots. I talk to amputees who are walking, ask them how it feels, and what advice they have for me to emulate their success. All the while, I believe in my heart that I am going to walk one day.

While I'm waiting for my bones to get strong enough for prosthetics, an active duty soldier visits me in my room. We click immediately — it feels like we've known each other forever, even though we've just met.

Then he blows my mind by telling me he's an amputee.

"Yo, you're an amputee?" I echo, not believing my eyes. He is so mobile, and he walks so well!

"Oh, man," he says, pulling up his pants leg, showing me his prosthetic. "You couldn't tell?"

My heart is leaping!

"Oh, bro," I say, "you're like an angel coming into my room showing me it's possible."

God is showing me direct evidence that what I believe in my heart is possible. It works! I pass the next DEXA test, and get up on my new prosthetic legs for the first time on November 4, 2012, in the Military Advanced Training Center (MATC) at Walter Reed National Military Medical Center.

The MATC is state-of-the-art and super high tech; they create customized prosthetics and provide top-of-the-line athletic equipment to help veterans regain the use of hands, arms, legs, feet, and much more.

As much as I believed in my heart this day would come, no fireworks exploded in the sky when it actually happened. The thought of standing on my legs had been just as real as the things I could touch. I had spent so much time thinking the thought — it wasn't like a moment of triumph — it was like *I've been here every single moment*. And that's how I am.

Despite my excitement and gratitude, the reality was that my new prosthetic legs were extremely painful! My prosthetist, Mike Corcoran, custom-made the legs to fit what remains below my left knee, and to provide a right knee and lower leg. The prosthetics have cups at the top to grip the flesh, so they stay in place while I'm walking.

And when I say grip, I mean *grip*.

In fact, when I first stand up, the pain is horrible, like I'm walking on my knees on hardwood or concrete floors.

I am stunned! I've been wishing and waiting, praying, and envisioning this moment. Now it's here, and the pain is excruciating! Every step is torture.

How am I gonna walk like this? How am I gonna run?

It felt like another breaking point. I mean, it would have been so easy to succumb to the pain and let it defeat me into quitting. I thought I was about to step into the promised land of walking and running. Yet it seemed unbearable.

Then I remembered books on success that I've read. They all say that the obstacle seems insurmountable when you first undertake anything. It flips on a voice in your head that shouts: *You've got no business being here. Let me show you how hard it's going to be.*

It might slam you down on the mat, but you are in the ring, and you are not going to go down like that. You are going to fight back, and you're going to stand on top of your opponent as the champion. Period. You have to believe this most when your doubts are trying to smack you down. So you have to flip your thinking. Take doubt as an affirmation that you will achieve your heart's desire. Imagine the doubt pummeling your mind, not as something that will hurt you, but something that will push you into the mental space where you can overcome the physical challenge.

For me, at the moment, it's pain.

When you start walking on prosthetics, it's like life is taunting: *No, you can't have this for free! You gotta work for this! And you gotta look stupid and overcome your doubt and insecurity and painful steps all by yourself. Oh, no, it's not going to be given to you for free!*

Normally on the first day, you would go into the practice room, put on the prosthetics, and spend 30 to 60 minutes walking back and forth, holding onto parallel bars with each hand for support. Typically, that's considered a full day. But not for me. I had waited too long to stop that soon. Instead, I keep learning to walk on my prosthetics for another hour on the parallel bars. I just keep going. I had been believing for months in my heart that I could be on my feet, and now that I am, no amount of pain or fatigue or soreness is going to sit me back down.

After two hours on the parallel bars, I ask to be hooked up to the harness so I can walk around the MATC track with two canes. I'm in pain. I'm tired. But I say, "You guys aren't gonna get me back in that chair."

If I could have taken my new legs out of the MATC, I would have, but protocol dictated that I leave my legs behind for the first few months. Once I was trained and stabilized, my legs were released to me. By then I knew that if I tried to walk on the legs I was born with — I wouldn't know how. I had re-trained my brain.

I had no comfort. I was forced to adapt. Forced to fight. That's what I want to cultivate in you: refuse to be denied! Fight for it!

Think about the alternative — going without it, failing to achieve your dreams, never learning to walk or run again. That alternative is not an option. It would mean the death of me inside. So I commit to figuring it out. Refusing to feel sorry for myself. Never boarding the pity party bus, because that's the express route to quitting, failure, and complete misery.

I want to win, and do things bigger and better than before.

Follow this example! Think about how, if I can rise up from such a dismal and seemingly impossible spot in that hospital bed when the doctor is telling me no, and my heart is telling me yes, then you can do it, too! Believe it! I guarantee you will amaze yourself.

TACKLING ANOTHER TOUGH ONE: SWIMMING

As I heal, the same competitive physical drive that inspired me to become a superfit Army Ranger leads me to the pool. I could have lived my whole life without ever swimming again, but I choose to swim and conquer it. I was a lifeguard in high school, and swimming is a good cardio workout. After a few days of putting it off, I finally summon the courage to get in the pool at Walter Reed.

This is not swimming!
This is me splashing water everywhere!

Without legs, swimming is all arms. It's *all* treading water. I have to find my feet fast! In the midst of this, the woman in charge of the pool comes over and says:

"Look, this is a 50-yard pool. You gotta go down and back and tread water for two minutes."

Before my injury: no problem. That would be an invitation to undertake a challenge, right then and there. I'd compete against myself and everybody in that pool. But now as I'm processing what she's telling me, I'm thinking, *I have no legs! Down and back? Tread water for two minutes? That's gonna be really hard. All arms!*

Then the lifeguard comes over and says: "You can't be here. Amputees come on Thursdays. Thursdays are Amputee Swim Day."

"Look, man," I say with a chuckle, thinking, *There's no way I'm getting out of this pool right now. I'm going to master this, now!* "You don't understand. It took all the courage I had today to get here and get in this pool. What do I have to do to stay in here today?"

"Swim up and back," the lifeguard says, "and tread water for two minutes."

Now, I have a choice. My head is saying, *I can't do this. It's all arms!* But my heart is declaring, *I want to do this! I am up for the challenge. I can do this! I will find my feet!*

In that moment, all my life's experiences say that despite having no experience swimming as an amputee, if my heart wants it, my head will just have to figure it out. My heart got me in the water. My head is now responsible for keeping me in it.

And I refuse to panic.

I take my knowledge about myself, my new body, and swimming, and I come up with a weak little sidestroke. After a few strokes, I figure out that if I put my head in the water, I can get a little buoyancy. Then I realize that if I keep my lungs inflated, I'm turning my body into more of a life raft.

I manage to get myself to the middle towards the deep end, and I start learning little tricks on how to stay afloat without exhausting my arms. Then I quickly discover how to swim with my new body. I can follow the black line down the lane, and if I stay to the right of it, I find a corridor between it and the lane buoys. If I remain within this range, I am swimming well!

Most people will not expose themselves to the embarrassment of flailing and splashing around until they figure out a new way to swim. So I'm telling you, just be okay with looking stupid as you learn on the fly. That's the only way to push past your breaking point and reach your Making Point.

This accomplishment in the pool gives me confidence to follow my heart's latest desire: sign up for a triathlon, which includes swimming nearly a mile!

Driving, walking, swimming. Check, check, check.

What about running? That's coming next…

How You Can Flex Your
Find-Your-Feet Muscle, Too

You've probably noticed that the way I think is the secret to my success. I've trained myself to flip the script on any bad feeling or situation, and think about it in a way that enables me get what I want.

If you take away anything from this book, remember: **every success or failure begins in your mind.** It's that simple. It's all about what you tell yourself.

When you set your mind on the right path, the universe will follow by blessing you with new people, opportunities, and dreams-coming-true — sometimes in ways that feel totally out of the blue. That's how I and my family have dined with presidents and met some of the top business leaders in the world.

And that's the only way I can explain how — after growing up in a trailer in North Carolina — I now live with my family in a beautiful, brand-new, custom built home that was provided to us by the Gary Sinise Foundation, which helps veterans. Its R.I.S.E. program — Restoring Independence Supporting Empowerment — constructs and donates smart homes for wounded veterans across America.

Dozens of people and several TV crews attended the dedication ceremony in February of 2017 in front of our house that was hidden behind a giant American flag. Several supporters spoke, and our home was unveiled.

You can watch a video of the event, which shows me walking and wheeling through the house and sitting on the bench in the shower, at GarySiniseFoundation.org/programs/rise.

Our home is as nice as those Khieda and I once dreamed about living in, back when we'd sneak into gated communities and fantasize about the beautiful mansions there. Now a home like that is our reality.

I stood at the podium, looking awestruck. "I didn't know it was going to be anything like this," I said, as Khieda, our daughters, my mother, my grandmother, and many relatives sat nearby. "I didn't know… it was going to be anything this nice. I didn't know it was going to be anything beyond my wildest dreams. Thank you so, so much. It means so much."

What are the odds?!

So now it's time to apply these messages to your life. Say you want to lose weight, get healthy, and get in shape. You've put it off for years and years, and you finally join a gym. But as you walk around, checking out the racks of dumbbells and rows of strength-training machines, you're intimidated, maybe even scared. You're probably confused about which machine works which muscle and where you should start. Plus, you're surrounded by physically fit people who are confidently pumping, twisting, running, and cycling. You may be tempted to run out of the gym and slip back to your comfort zone at home on the couch.

But that will only keep you stuck. I'm here to tell you, the only way to change is to take action. And start small. Start at one. Don't set out to run a marathon on day one. Just find the willpower within yourself to get up off the couch and go to the gym or to go for a walk. It will require one hour from your day, and that investment in yourself will make the other 23 hours feel so much better. If you're trying to improve your diet, you don't have to become an all-organic vegetarian overnight. Just make incremental changes, such as, "I won't eat candy at my desk. I'll snack on fresh fruit instead."

This activates your find-your-feet muscle. What you see everyday triggers your mind to think a certain way. So, cover your vision board with everything you can imagine that you want in life. Put it in a spot where you'll see it every morning or all day long. Pray over it. Meditate and envision yourself doing whatever the vision board shows: getting fit, learning to walk or talk or feed yourself again; feeling happy and peaceful; finding your soulmate; driving your dream car. The possibilities are limitless. Go for it!

Think about how you can activate your find-your-feet muscle

and make it stronger every day. Write about it in a journal. You know yourself best, so write out a strategy that works best for you. Refuse to indulge your inner critic; silence that negative voice inside your head so you can encourage yourself to become your best you.

IMPROVISE

Life is constantly changing, for better or for worse.

The key to adapting is realizing that whatever happened in the past was a gift. And whatever is happening now is also a gift.

A good attitude has to be the one constant in the equation.

Too many folks maintain the mindset that they'll keep a positive attitude when circumstances are good. When circumstances are bad, their attitude follows suit. These fair-weather feelings are a recipe for disaster. On the other hand, a positive attitude right now will help you win, no matter what the weather is like any given day, no matter when your taxes are due, no matter who wins an election, and no matter what your income is right now.

Change your mind; change your life.

To do this, you have to improvise. You have to make do with whatever your situation is right now. In the military, we had to improvise a lot. Imagine just how sweaty grown men can get while marching under the blazing desert sun in 120-degree heat wearing 50 pounds of gear. We needed to take showers. But the outpost in Afghanistan had no showers. We didn't stand around complaining. We improvised, by rigging water bottles over our heads. It was as close to a shower as we could get, and it did the job.

So, rather than dwell on how bad an obstacle seems, redirect your thoughts into a brainstorm that flashes up some creative solutions to get what you want.

CELEBRATE THE SMALL SUCCESSES

Learning to drive, swim, walk, run... I didn't start off mastering any of this.

I screeched, splashed, stumbled, and fell. I grimaced in pain. I questioned how in the world I would ever become good at any of these activities. How would I overcome the physical pain and embarrassment of not mastering these things like I had done everything in my past?

By celebrating the small successes. Taking three steps without wobbling. Taking off in a short sprint on my blades. Changing swim lanes flawlessly with hand paddles. Doing one perfect swim stroke, and loving that smooth gliding motion through the water.

Man, the excitement of those little moments is like a tank full of rocket fuel to propel you to work hard and keep improving. When I eventually climbed Stone Mountain in Georgia, it was step by step, boulder by boulder. You can't climb the mountain in one step. You do it gradually, and when you feel good about every inch you ascend — and celebrate the times you fall, but get back up and keep going — you will be unstoppable!

HOW TO ENGAGE YOUR FIND-YOUR-FEET MUSCLE

Here are some questions for you to define your life changes and explore how you can re-train your brain to see them differently.

What life change have you experienced that feels like a road block? What potential positives can you see in your situation?

_____

_____

_____

_____

How can you cultivate patience with yourself as you overcome the anger and frustration that are a natural part of major life changes?

_____

_____

_____

_____

Write down a dialogue between your head and your heart that will put your heart in charge.

_____

_____

_____

_____

What mantra can you tell yourself in the moment to transform from hopelessness to a belief that you can succeed?

_____

_____

_____

_____

What does your find-your-feet muscle look like? What triggers you to flex it? What weakens it? This could be fear, criticism, or the pain of past failures. What can you tell yourself to leave the mental blocks in the past and focus on flexing like never before?

_____

_____

_____

_____

Describe yourself and your life when you use your find-your-feet muscle to maximum capacity. How do you feel?

_____

_____

_____

_____

What new good things are happening in your life? Make this your goal. Read it every day, believe it, and become your best self!

_____

_____

_____

_____

4

Persevering Through the Pain

"Blessed is the one who perseveres under trial because, having stood the test, that person will receive the crown of life that the Lord has promised to those who love him."

James 1:12

THE PAIN FEELS LIKE flames flickering under the stumps where my legs once were. I've already run 17 miles, and the skin is broken and bleeding inside the cuffs attached to my prosthetic running blades.

But I can't stop running.

Because 21 months ago — when I was sitting in my hospital bed with no legs, watching TV coverage of double amputee Oscar Pistorius compete against able-bodied runners in the Olympics — I decided that Master Sergeant Cedric King would one day do the same.

Now I'm doing it. I'm not in the Olympics. I'm running the Boston Marathon — one of the world's oldest and most prestigious marathons. Just like Oscar, my amputated legs are replaced by metal blades that look like flat hooks; they make a *tap* sound every time they hit the concrete streets of this historic city.

I'm among 30,000 men and women — most of whom have two legs — who are tackling the 26.2-mile course. All around us on the sidewalks, a half million people, including pretty college women who are screaming cheers and asking runners to kiss them along a whole mile of the route, are cheering us on.

Every year the race is held on Patriots' Day, a state holiday that celebrates victories in the American Revolution. The sun is shining. It's an unseasonably warm 75 degrees, and the city is jubilantly celebrating its perseverance through pain and fear. One year ago, on April 15, 2013, terrorists' bombs exploded at the finish line, killing three people and injuring hundreds of others.

At that exact moment, I was at the MATC with my physical therapist and prosthetist, as they helped me try my running blades for the first time. As we watched the aftermath of Boston's horrendous tragedy unfold on live TVs, my heart ached for the victims. But my spirit leapt with the overwhelming desire to do something for the survivors and victims. I wanted them to see that I didn't allow my injuries to stop me, and that this bombing didn't have to steal their dreams either.

In the MATC, these thoughts bombarded my mind as I slip my legs into the cuffs of my blades for the first time. I can't wait to take off running! Before my injury, running was so easy. I could do a six-minute mile effortlessly, leading hundreds of soldiers on long runs, calling out motivational cadences for miles.

Now, as I get used to the feeling of my blades, excitement surges through me. My new running legs feel as light as feathers compared to my walking prosthetics.

I will be running again in no time! Thank you, Lord!

My therapist Mike hooks me up to a harness attached to ropes and a ceiling grid that keep me upright and balanced on the blades as I stand on the physical therapy track.

I take off running at top speed! Oh, my goodness, it feels *so* good to move fast. This is the first time I've run in almost a year, and it becomes one of the best moments of my life since losing my legs. Excitement and gratitude overwhelm me, as does hope that every amputee in the world can experience this feeling. All the while, I am deeply affected by news reports about the Boston bombing.

I have to help them! Someday, I'll show my support by running the Boston Marathon.

"I'm ready!" I say.

Mike unhooks me from the rope. I immediately fall down. And that begins part two of Master Sergeant Cedric King learning to walk again. Running is faster and more aggressive on your limbs, with a lot more impact. It hurts my bones because they are not used to such impact. And going that fast again is scary.

No surprise, I fall a lot at first. But no matter how bruised and banged up I get, I am as fearless as a two-year-old who's learning to run. That toddler doesn't think about how hard the floor is, where the wall is, or where the couch is. That toddler just wants to move, with speed and adventure. Same with me, but every time I take a jogging step, I teeter. Crashing and falling soon follow.

Still, I am determined to master the art of walking, jogging, and running. I will do the Boston Marathon.

Shortly after the bombing, a group of amputees from Walter Reed is chosen to visit the bombing survivors. I desperately want to go, but I'm not selected for the trip. I'm a bit devastated, but I understand that God was teaching me patience to sit back and wait for my turn, which could be bigger and better than the opportunity I think I'm missing. So, I channel my disappointment into determination to push harder to somehow become part of the survivors' lives.

I remember some scripture from Bible school. James 1:12 reads: "Blessed is the one who perseveres under trial because, having stood the test, that person will receive the crown of life that the Lord has promised to those who love him."

For me, that crown would be the medal that race officials would put around my neck at the finish line of the Boston Marathon. It would symbolize the culmination of my perseverance under trial to show the world that if a double amputee can run 26.2 miles, then nothing is impossible.

Little did I know just how excruciatingly painful that trial would be.

TEAMWORK MAKES THE DREAM WORK: LEARNING TO RUN AGAIN

I'm going to be running 10 miles next year.

I started repeating that mantra nonstop in August of 2012, just a month after my injury, when the doc said running within a year was "too high a goal" that "nobody" could achieve.

Just setting a goal and declaring my desire to run — even though I was confined to a bed and a wheelchair — inspired others, including the wife of US Defense Secretary Ash Carter. He and his wife Stephanie came to visit Walter Reed most weekends, and just a few weeks after my injury, I told them that I wanted to run again.

"I'm getting ready to run the Chicago Marathon," Stephanie Carter told me.

"I'm going to do that someday," I said.

"Well, when I'm there," she said, "I'm going to keep you in my thoughts and that's going to be a motivation." Later, Stephanie shared that she ran with her business partner and told him about how motivating and inspiring I was for her.

"When we passed the marker for mile 10," she said, "I asked my business partner, 'You know who would be able to run 10 miles? Cedric! So, we're going to get this done!'"

Since then, I have become good friends with Stephanie and Ash.

"I'm sure that Cedric is an uplifting spirit for his fellow soldiers," Stephanie says now. "He's in a better position to inspire and motivate people who are facing the same kinds of challenges. One of the biggest determinants in life is not your intellect or talent, but your resilience. He's exhibited that from the first meeting. Some people give you the thousand-mile stare and you wonder how you're going to navigate it all. He stood out when his arm had pins and braces; he was so banged up the first time we saw him. But he was just as bubbly as he is now. We just hold a place in our hearts for Cedric."

My initial visits with Stephanie and Ash enabled me to share my dream of running again one day. But as James 26:2 reads in the Bible: "Faith without works is dead." You can have all the faith in the world, but if you don't take action, nothing will happen.

So, I put in the work of mastering my running blades, and relied on the belief that teamwork makes the dream work. In high school, I played basketball on a team. In the Army, I was part of a platoon. Being on the best team helps you win the game and triumph in battle. It motivates you to play harder and do your best. In war, it saves your life and the lives of the people you're fighting to protect.

As you battle to overcome your obstacles, you need teammates who will support you, encourage you, and make you stronger.

Thankfully, Khieda is the captain, coach, and cheerleader for Team Cedric, for everything I do, including my quest to run again. As such, she became my first running partner. Of course, being a super-tough soldier who dominated the most grueling physical fitness competitions in the Army, I wanted to run a mile right out of the gate. But I didn't understand how to maneuver on running blades outside of the therapy room. Nor did I realize how difficult it would be to balance or climb hills. So, on my first run, I was lucky to do a third of a mile.

"Let's take it slow," Khieda said.

"No, I want to be fast!" I said. "I want to outrun you!"

"You are so competitive!" she teased. Then she sprinted away.

I tried to catch her. But she dusted me.

Determined to win, I challenged, "Let's do another lap."

My wife left me in the dust once again. That motivated me to work hard, and soon we were taking longer and longer runs. That prepared me for my first official race that showed just how big and loving my team really is.

Inspired by my handwritten note shortly after I awoke from the coma, my mother helped organize the Run Warrenton: Walk, Run, Scoot 5K in April of 2013, just weeks after the Boston bombing.

Nearly 300 people — out of just 850 residents in the whole town! — showed up for Warrenton's first-ever 5K. It was unlike anything that our small town had ever experienced. Former classmates, teachers, neighbors, family members, fellow soldiers from Fort Bragg, and strangers united to celebrate the miracle of my survival and determination to succeed against the odds stacked against a double amputee.

I wasn't ready to run on my blades, so I wore my prosthetic legs and used canes to walk the three-mile race route through town. People who finished before me lined the streets to shout cheers and shed tears as I passed by. At my sides the whole time were some of my friends from grade school and Fort Bragg. My cousin Vydashon and my mom were on hand, too.

My mom playfully recalls the day by saying, "I think I was 'mothering' him too much in front of his crew, so he told me to go on and he would catch up sometime later."

After the race, people stood in a long line that wrapped around the courthouse square; I greeted every single person and heard over and over that the day felt more like a family reunion or a community celebration than a race.

All their love and kind words deposited deep inside me, enriching my spirit and strengthening my mind and body to keep pushing toward bigger and bigger goals.

The run in my hometown was also known as the Wounded Warriors Race, raising funds for the Wounded Warrior Project, which helps injured veterans. It has become an annual event, attracting 230 participants in 2014. The following year was extra special because it was during the 20-year high school reunion for the class of 1995. A lot of my classmates ran the 5K with us that morning. In 2016, about 200 people signed up, but unfortunately this was the only one I missed because I was recovering from the Boston Marathon a few weeks prior.

The "team" of supporters united by our annual race helps veterans across America, and that first year especially helped push me to achieve my mantra:

I'm going to be running 10 miles next year.

After the run in Warrenton and for the rest of 2013, I trained hard, using both my prosthetic legs and my running blades. Then I put my progress to the test by running the Disney Half Marathon in January of 2014. The race got hard at mile 12, but I made it to the finish line. That was exhilarating! I exceeded my mantra of running 10 miles!

The day after the race, we went to Disney World. I was in a wheelchair, and I saw a man wearing six medals around his neck.

"What did you do?" I asked in awe.

"I did the full marathon circuit," he said. "It's called the Disney Marathon Series: a 5K, a 10K, a half marathon, and a full marathon in four days."

"I want to do that!" I exclaimed, vowing to achieve that goal in 2015.

I would try the Disney series in a year, but in the meantime another goal was beckoning: the Boston Marathon in April of 2014. This elite race attracts the best runners from around the world. Participants must qualify to race. For someone like me, I had to qualify with a time between six and eight hours.

Thankfully, the folks at the Scott Rigsby Foundation, which helps wounded veterans participate in races, sponsored my participation and registered me for the marathon.

My plan was to train hard for the next three months, preferably by running outdoors during Bethesda's mild winter weather. The best running conditions for me were just like in the Army: wide open spaces with long-distance routes. But Mother Nature did not cooperate. She struck metropolitan Washington, DC with a vengeance: frigid temperatures, endless snowfall, and iced-over streets. I was so determined to train, that I tried running on ice while wearing my blades. I'll spare you the gory details of what a bad idea that was.

I considered my indoor options. The tiny track at Walter Reed would force me to run 13 laps to total one mile — and 340-plus laps for the full marathon! Training for a 26.2-mile race by running in circles sounded dreadful!

My next option? The treadmill. But balancing on a moving surface while wearing my running blades was so hard! I just could not figure it out. And let me tell you, getting thrown off the treadmill is scary. It's like being in a car without brakes. All you can do is brace for a crash. I tried several times, but the conveyor belt kept propelling me backwards.

"Forget it!" I exclaimed after crashing to the floor once again. "Amputees don't do this! I'm not doing it anymore!"

The act of giving up was like jumping out of the positive, faithful, action-oriented dimension where my heart, mind, and body normally dwelled. I soon found myself in a free-fall into enemy territory: the couch. Yes, I was a tough Army Ranger who had survived battlefields in war zones and life threatening conditions during Ranger School. But the cozy comfort of the couch is an extreme danger zone that can easily claim the most ambitious, optimistic person.

Why suffer through grueling workouts in snow and ice or the monotony of a tiny track, when I could kick back with my wife, eating Oreos and jelly rolls, while binge-watching *Breaking Bad*? I already had to leave our apartment at Walter Reed for my endless doctors' appointments, physical therapy sessions, and countless surgeries. So, on top of that burden, why struggle on running blades and risk my life on the treadmill, when I could be playing it safe by sitting in a movie theatre with Khieda, and going to lunch for our "Date Days" while the girls were at school? And why do anything after that, when I could plunk back down on the couch, eating all my favorite snacks while watching more TV?

> *Boy, you better be training,* my inner voice kept warning. *You better do something. If you stay on the couch for a week, it can turn into two weeks, then a month. You're running out of time to prepare for this marathon.*

Most people train four or five months before running 26.2 miles. Now I had less than three months, and I had done nothing. The couch had become a powerful magnet, pulling me deeper into negativity and inactivity. Guilt consumed me as time ticked relentlessly toward race day: April 21. Every time I saw the date on my phone, a burning sensation of dread flared my gut. In the back of my mind, I knew that procrastination had become a bully, but I just couldn't find the strength to stand up and fight back.

No, I just sat there taking my self-inflicted beating of guilt and worry. Still, I could not snap out of it. Nor could I get up off the couch — and train.

So, when it came time to go to Boston for race day, despite all the enthusiasm I had felt about helping the people of Boston recover from the terrorist attack, I knew I was in big, big trouble.

RUNNING THE BOSTON MARATHON

Now I'm here, and every step is excruciating. My lungs are burning. My heart is hammering. Somehow I've made it to Mile 17, but finishing this race seems like an impossible feat.

Still, I cannot abandon my mission to show support for the people here. I'm wearing a yellow T-shirt in honor of Martin William Richard, an eight-year-old boy from Boston, who had been watching the race with his family when the second bomb killed him. My running guide, Scott Johnson, is also wearing the T-shirt, emblazoned with *MWR8*, and we are keeping his spirit alive. I qualified to participate in the race thanks to the Scott Rigsby Foundation teaming up with the Martin Richard Foundation. Their fundraisers enabled Martin's parents to honor their son by building Martin's Park at Children's Wharf in Boston.

I feel that I'm making a difference. Likewise, I have befriended bombing survivors Patrick Downes and Jessica Kensky, who were newlyweds when they each lost their left legs. I met them the night before the marathon at a special event. We hit it off, and it was an honor to share my story and encourage them to persevere through their pain.

As a result, my heart is happy, but my body is giving out. Unfortunately, my brain is following right behind my body, under assault by "the noise." That's what I call extreme pain when it becomes so horrible that it becomes white noise, like static in my head, and it's hard to think about anything else.

The noise blasts open the doors to extremely negative thoughts. It enrages my inner critic, which screams at me like the loudest drill sergeant ever: *Cedric, you didn't train! You didn't respect the race! What were you thinking? Running the Boston Marathon without training!?*

It's been agony since the starting line. I struggled through the first four miles, but the noise attacks at Mile 13.

Alright, I tell myself, *it's not the end of the world. I'm not dead. I can probably make it.*

I keep pushing, and here I am battling to find the strength to keep running. The pain consumes my mind along with a barrage of questions:

How did this happen? How did I fail to train after giving up so easily when faced with the challenges of weather, treadmill mishaps, and refusal to run on an indoor track? Why was I so quick to take myself out of the game? Why hadn't I honored my commitment to myself to be my best at all times? How had I abandoned my Army Ranger Creed, whose commitment is emblazoned on my soul?

Words that I recited every morning play in my mind as my running blades tap amid the deep rumble of countless running shoes around me. The cheering, the music, the excitement — none of it can drown out the anger and disappointment that I feel toward myself for defying my soldier's code of conduct.

"Energetically will I meet the enemies of my country," the Ranger Creed says. "I shall defeat them on the field of battle for I am better trained and will fight with all my might. Surrender is not a Ranger word."

Today, I am not better trained. I had surrendered to negativity, laziness, and procrastination. And I am here to defy the enemies of our country who had planted two homemade bombs at the finish line one year ago to kill, maim, and terrorize Americans. This race today, and my participation in it, represent the same fight that I had endured during my three deployments in the Middle East.

"…and under no circumstances will I ever embarrass my country," the Creed says.

At the moment, I feel embarrassed for myself, for failing to train and do my best in this show of support for this city and our country. That thought seems amplified by the deep chop of the Apache helicopters above as the National Guard patrols the marathon route from the sky. I have to keep running. This race means too much to America for me to give up.

The pain is telling me otherwise. Before the race kicked off, the Scott Rigsby Foundation folks explained our "escape plan." If it gets too tough, they said, our guides could call a golf cart, which would pick us up anywhere between the starting line and Mile 13, so we can stop running and be driven to the finish line.

Man, you gotta be kidding me! I thought at the time. *I'm not about to let you take me to the finish line and act like I've been running the whole time!*

However now, facing a big hill at Mile 17, that escape plan is starting to look really good. The problem is that — because security is extremely high — the course is on lockdown after Mile 13; you can't return to the course from the outside after that point.

I am stuck! But all I think is, *Get me out of pain! Find me something with four wheels, immediately!*

However, I don't tell Scott, because he'll tell me not to quit. As my guide, Scott Johnson is accompanying me throughout the race to make sure that I'm okay. He's with me, thanks to the nonprofit organization, Achilles International, which pairs guides with people who have disabilities so we can participate in races across America. Scott is also my coach, and he doesn't let me off easily.

The sight of a power-gel station sparks a flicker of hope. Maybe a jolt of carbs from the little packet will help me power through. Especially since we're about to start running up the brutally steep Newton Hills. The hardest part of this marathon is at the end — over five straight miles of unrelenting incline. It's deceiving because a long downhill stretch precedes these hills.

This is where a lot of runners quit.

Yes! I've been waiting for this! I feel so grateful for the relief of running downhill. But at the bottom, you hit that first hill. And you climb and you climb and you climb. I'm like, *God, why?*

That's the first of four more hills in Newton, between Miles 18 and 21. Even the most experienced runners get eaten alive here. They call it "hitting the wall" — when runners feel that they cannot take another step. It's the breaking point. But it's actually the Making Point.

And believe me, there's a very fine line between the two.

MY BREAKING POINT? OR MY MAKING POINT?

We pass Mile 17, but a short time after that, finishing this marathon still seems impossible.

I can't think of anything that would make it worthwhile to endure to the end. Not the glory and satisfaction of running a full marathon less than two years after losing my legs. Not becoming the first double amputee from Walter Reed to run a marathon. Not having the race officials place a medal around my neck. Not having my picture taken or video shot by all the people — including a thousand journalists from the around the world — at the finish line. Everything seems so insignificant.

"Keep going!" people cheer from the sidelines. "You're the best!"

I feel worse, pressured to feel that I have to finish. Plus, the motivation of people cheering is external. It helps, but to truly succeed, you need an internal cheering section. It comes from your own fortitude, your belief in yourself, and your belief that God is propelling you forward with strength you don't know you have.

At the moment, the pain is so terrible, the noise drowns out my internal cheering section. I sit down on the curb, contemplating whether I can continue. I record that moment on my phone's camera with the goal of posting the video on Facebook, where Khieda, the girls, their teachers, their school, our family, and our friends are watching me across America. All they have to do is punch my number into the computer, and a computer chip on my bib enables them to zoom into my exact location, thanks to cameras along the entire route.

"Right now I'm hurting so, so bad!" I say into my phone's camera.

"No, he's not," Scott says over my shoulder. "He's gonna get this damn thing done, and don't listen to a word he says. He's totally stoned on Gatorade."

I say into my phone, "This is one of those times when I gotta figure it out. It sucks! I think we're at Mile 18. Something crazy. We have a little ways to go. The closer we get, the tougher it gets. But we'll get there though."

Somehow I find the strength to stand up and run again. A short time later, I step into the medical tent, along with Scott and two women who are running together.

"What can we get you?" the volunteers ask. "Would you like water?"

These people give out bananas and orange slices, Vaseline, Band Aids, Gatorade, and towels. Medical personnel also help anyone who needs their attention. At this point, it's easy to feel sorry for yourself, throw a pity party, and invite all these friendly people to join in.

Everyone in the tent is super nice. It's the opposite of the military. It occurs to me that the medical tent would be better if some big, loud sergeant were in there making people do push-ups. I really believe that sometimes when we're in the worst places of our lives, we need somebody kicking us in our butts. Otherwise, we'll never know how strong we are.

The two ladies who entered with us are watching me. Scott encourages me to keep going, so we head back onto the course, and up the seemingly endless hills for the next three miles. Somehow I make it up and over four hills, but I'm in agony.

"This is Heartbreak Hill," Scott says. "The last of the hills. This is the hardest one."

"Bro, it can't be any harder than what we just went through," I say, noticing a guy at the bottom of the hill. He's banging a gong, over and over. The deep boom echoes ominously through the crowd. It's like a movie scene.

What in the world?!

I run right past the guy. Halfway up this hill, I'm breathing so hard, it feels like I'm suffocating. And there's no end in sight. This incline seems to go on forever. I can see the top, but it feels like I'm not moving. It feels like a mind game. I'm giving 100 percent! Any other time in life, it seems like I get to see some result for this kind of effort. But this time, *nothing*! It's like running on an uphill treadmill, going nowhere.

Gasping for breath, grimacing from the pain in my legs, I feel overwhelmed with frustration. It's going to take a miracle for me to finish this race.

GIVE YOUR ALL TO MAKE MIRACLES

In order for life to give you a miracle, it asks for only one thing:

EVERYTHING YOU'VE GOT!

It's very simple.

"Give, and it shall be given unto you," reads Luke 6:38 in the Bible.

So, what are you giving during those tough times when you're begging God for a miracle? Are you giving your all? Are you giving all you have?

A lot of times, we give *some* — and expect big results in exchange.

When I started to learn to walk, I could do 10 minutes. I'd be in pain and out of breath. But during that, I remembered the only way I had achieved anything great in the past was when I told myself, "Just give all you have." So, I gave it my all. That mindset enabled me to push my body, and I began to walk for longer stretches. I knew that the miracle would come when I began to give all that I have, because God would recognize my efforts, and more would be given. Now I walk 90 percent of my day on my legs.

Unfortunately, it's human nature to just give *some* of what we have, then still expect the miracle. If you're looking for a great example of how to overcome this, watch babies. They give their absolute all! They're focusing all their energy on going from crawling to running in just a few months. They work so hard, and play so hard, they fall asleep in the middle of the living room.

Now as I struggle to survive the final stretch of the Boston Marathon, I think about the miraculous feat of the human body's ability to run 26.2 miles from the starting line to the finish line. About 30,000 people around me are proving that it is possible.

But it feels impossible for me.

The contract that we have with life says this: *I'll give you the impossible… when you give me all you have.* You fall into a breach of contract so many times. At the end of the day, you put your head on your pillow expecting miracles to happen, when you're in breach of contract because you did not give all you have. You're thinking life did you wrong, or that life is not fair.

Life is still fair. Life wants you to know that it will be totally responsible for its part of the deal, when you become totally responsible for your part of the deal. Your part of this contract with fate is like a seed. Your job is to plant the seed. There's nothing you can do to make a leaf or an apple. You have to rely on faith and God to make the plant come out of the seed. That's God's role in the contract. He produces the miracle, when you plant the seed, water it, and provide the sunlight.

Less than two years after doctors said it would be highly unlikely for me to run anytime soon, I completed the Boston Marathon in April of 2014. The 26.2 mile race enabled me to prove to myself that I can achieve anything, and that if I can do the impossible, then you can, too. I also participated to illustrate perseverance in the wake of a deadly terrorist bombing at the finish line in 2013. I have participated in the Boston Marathon every year since, and in 2017 I competed on a bike. Photo Credit: Joseph Kelley.

Then when you are giving it your all to nurture this seed, you have to depend on the miracle to do its part of the contract. We think that the secret to making miracles happen is to beg, borrow, steal, cut a side deal, meet the right people, and pay a little bit every month.

No!

All you have to do… is ALL you CAN do.

Then the stress or worry or frustration evaporates. You can sleep in peace when you know you gave your everything. You can sleep in peace when you earned an honest day's pay in the job of your life. Because if you don't, you're robbing yourself of the riches that come after you've invested every ounce of your being into what you want.

Giving your all is GIVING YOUR BEST. And only you really know when you're giving your best. Recently I was at the gym with my cousin, Kenya Solomon, who is one of my closest friends. We grew up together, and we are inseparable. That means we work out together, too, and he competes with me.

So a short while ago, we were at the gym, and Kenya's arms were buckling before he hit 25 push-ups. For me, push-ups are super easy. I can do hundreds. For a moment, I had a superior attitude about his ability compared to mine.

"Dude, you can do more!" I say. "It's easy!"

But Kenya's 25 push-ups look like they're hurting so bad, like they would be his breaking point. Still, he keeps pushing hard on those shaky arms. He grimaces. Groans. And keeps pushing!

Then I realize, Kenya is giving it his ALL! His all is different than my all. Now he is giving it! And guess what? He keeps pushing and pushing until finally, 25 push-ups become easy.

This is not typical. Too many times, we're not giving everything. I love that story in the Bible where people are coming to Jesus with offerings. People are dumping money, jewelry, and diamonds, when a lady comes along with two pennies. Jesus stops, staring in awe at the lady with two pennies. Everybody wonders why he's impressed when she gave so little in comparison to the riches they were giving.

And Jesus says, "She gave more than all of you combined."

"She only gave two pennies," they say. "What do you mean?"

"It's not the amount of what she gave," Jesus responds. "It's that those two pennies were 100 percent of everything she owns. She gave me her all."

She had not declared this. She didn't have to, because Jesus knew her heart — and rewarded her for it. Likewise, in life, we are the only ones who know what our 100 percent looks like.

It looks and feels like our breaking point. But a lot of people are afraid to get to the place where they buckle. That, however, is where you'll find the miracle. That is the Making Point.

PUSHING PAST YOUR RED LINE TO GET YOUR MIRACLES

I had been running nearly nine hours on stumps that hurt beyond belief.

Climbing hills. Panting for breath. Cursing myself for not training, not respecting this huge challenge, not even allowing the patriotic motivation for my involvement to inspire me to get off the couch to prepare for this.

But I'm in it now. And I have to stay in the fire and take the heat. I will not quit!

I kept telling myself this during those final, seemingly impossible miles of the Boston Marathon. I was way beyond the cardio burn that I always sought when running in the military.

I call it my "red line." That's a reference to the 1982 Ford Pinto that my mom drove when I was a kid. The engine revved super high, because the RPMs surged into the red, white, and orange zones, every time she shifted a gear. Meanwhile, the car was noisy and belched a lot of smoke. It was so embarrassing!

"Mom, what's wrong with this car?" I would ask.

"Nothing," she'd say. "It's just trying to get to the next gear!"

In the Army, when I was trying to get better at something, I had to hit my own little red line. At the time, I couldn't run two miles under 11 minutes for the Army Physical Fitness Test, which measured our cardiovascular fitness, endurance, and muscle strength. Every soldier could score a maximum of 100 points in each of the categories of push-ups, sit-ups, and a two-mile run. I always aimed for a perfect score of 300, but my slow running made that impossible. In fact, for a long time, my time was around 12:20. I was stuck!

When training, I'd stop before it became painful. I never reached the point of agony. Then, along came a day when I was competing with someone else. I wanted to win so badly! And that desire helped me push past the agony, and past the pain.

My body was like my mom's car. I was giving everything I had to reach that red line and shift up into my highest gear. And as soon as I allowed myself to be uncomfortable for an extended period, I started running 11-minute miles consistently. As a result, I improved on the PT test and ultimately scored perfect 300s. After that, I never dropped below 300. If I were to take the test today, I believe my high degree of physical fitness would still enable me to score 300 — even without my legs.

Unfortunately, a lot of us quit when it starts to hurt. We give up before we get to that red line. For the car, the red line is bad. For people, the red line is good. When I hit my personal red line in Boston, I became that Pinto, struggling to persevere through the pain. I wanted the miracle of finishing the race!

Even though, at Mile 22, my stumps are numb.

God, how can I possibly run four more miles? I have to focus on one mile at a time. One step at a time. But I'm losing power. My Garmin activity tracker is dead because the battery ran out. My cell phone is about to run out of juice. And I feel like the agony is killing part of me. It's taking my eyes off the finish line and forcing me to focus on the pain. I want to stop running and walk to the end.

"Hey, we're done already," my inner critic is saying.

No! I answer. *This is where we have to pour it on. This is the time to put the same amount of effort as Mile 1 and 17 and 22. You gave those 100 percent, so don't rob this last part of effort.*

My body, however, hasn't received this "Keep Going" alert from my mind. I'm convinced that my legs are incapable of running four more miles. At that moment of mental defeat, my phone rings.

"Oh my God, you're doing it!" Khieda shrieks. "I'm so impressed! I'm so proud of you!"

I remember that Amari and Khamya are watching a live stream of my race with their teacher; in fact, their entire school is watching and cheering for me. So are my friends, family, and people all over the country.

For the next three minutes, Khieda goes on and on about how strong I am, how tough I am, how courageous I am. Her enthusiasm bursts through the phone like rocket fuel, and my body responds accordingly.

Khieda's call is divine intervention. God spoke to me through my wife. He provided a power boost in the form of enthusiasm from her and our children. Life speaks the language of enthusiasm. It makes your heart skip a beat. You light up. Your heart flutters. Your mind soars. And energy jolts through your body.

That happens during this phone call when I suddenly feel euphoric, thinking, *I'm doing something that my wife didn't think I could do; something I didn't even know I could do.*

Now if you're thinking, "Well of course your wife is proud of you. What's the big deal?" The big deal is that it's hard to impress your spouse. You usually have to do something over and above.

That's why her pride makes all the pain in my legs worth it. God knows that I need her encouragement right now, that I'm accomplishing something that defies her beliefs. All this love exploding in my brain and heart shoots down through my body to propel me through those last four miles.

GETTING MY MIRACLE AT THE FINISH LINE

Having a clear picture of the finish line — which I snapped with my cell phone the day before and have meditated on many times since — helps me believe that I can get there. The last two-tenths of a mile is this iconic stretch down Boylston Street.

It's lined by crowds cheering so loudly, it's almost deafening. But all I want to do is finish. Then I realize, you have to respect the last two-tenths of a mile, like any part of the race. Sometimes, by disrespecting the last few 100 yards, we minimize the moment by rushing through it. We miss it.

Suddenly as I'm coming down the street, I'm overwhelmed with emotion. Tears sting my eyes. The last time I had cried was when Khieda gave me news that my legs had been amputated. Now I'm crying tears of relief. Joy. Gratitude to God for blessing me with this miracle.

Because I am running across the finish line!

I'm doing the impossible!

I persevered through the pain, and am now rewarded with this miracle.

I believe in God's realm, there's an Office of Blessings for people who are persevering through the pain. That office is always looking for people who have made up their minds to keep on marching, no matter how bad things get. It rewards their perseverance with blessings beyond belief.

The Boston Marathon taught me that nothing is impossible. My life's duty is to keep proving that to myself, and to the world, so that **you** can find this inner strength and accomplish anything. Suddenly I understand the "why" behind my injury. God is teaching me these huge lessons and is using me as a teaching tool to help you find your miracles.

FEELING UNSTOPPABLE — AND FAILING!

A month after Boston, I feel invincible. I'm taking college courses, and crushing every assignment and test. I have left all possibility of failure in the dust, and want to conquer more seemingly impossible goals with ease.

So, I sign up for the Ironman triathlon in Raleigh in the spring of 2014. An Ironman competition is 70.3 miles of swimming, bike riding, and running. More specifically, it's a 1.2-mile swim, a 56-mile bike ride, and a 13.1-mile half marathon.

I'm gonna go out there and destroy it!

I do the swim. But once I get on that bike, I realize, I haven't respected it. I had wrongly assumed that the gears would make it easier than running. Plus, I was so arrogant about my athletic prowess, that I borrowed my buddy's bike. Serious triathletes actually have special bikes that are fitted to their bodies.

Remember my greatest fears in Boston? That my body would give out? That I would have to do something I never did? That I would quit!?

Well, when I hit Mile 35 on that bike, I collapse. I literally fall off the bike while pedaling up a hill. I don't want to quit, but pedaling truly has become impossible.

Meanwhile, the time keeper, who rides along the route in a truck, is about to run over me. Luckily he's paying attention, sees me, and stops.

"Hey man, you okay?" he asks.

I'm so dehydrated, I can barely talk. But somehow I say, "No, I'm gonna keep going."

"Okay," he says, trying to help me stand back up. But I can't go any further.

"Hey, dude," he says. "I gotta pull you. You're not making any progress."

I get on the bike. Fall off again.

And I'm done!

Race officials want to cut off my wristband, which contains a chip to track my times and indicates that I'm registered.

"No, keep it on there," I tell them. I want the wristband to serve as a constant reminder that yes, I failed, but I'll give 1,000 percent of myself to train for another Ironman competition — and finish!

That wristband is not coming off, I promise myself, *until I finish a half Ironman.* That bracelet stays on my wrist for the next five months! I don't remove it until September when, thanks to the Scott Rigsby Foundation, I have the opportunity to do a half Ironman. This time, cameras from HBO follow me throughout the competition.

You have to dominate the swim! I tell myself. *You have to dominate the run!*

I'm doing fine on the bike until I hit the point where I collapsed the first time. At Mile 35, I start feeling nervous. I don't know if I can make it past there, like Mile 17 in Boston.

A voice inside me taunts, "Hey, this is where you broke down last time. You've never done 56 miles on a bike!" While training, I had done 40 miles on the bike to prepare for this.

And now it hurts so bad! The problem is, my bones are still growing and as a result they push through the flesh where my legs were amputated, and that's extremely painful, especially when I'm putting constant pressure and pounding in athletic competitions. On top of that, I'm only working with one hamstring and have to pedal with my quadriceps.

By the grace of God, I finish the bike ride. Then, during the transition from the bike to the run, as I put on my running blades, it's like, *This is now officially agony. This could not be harder!* It's so difficult to watch all the other competitors finish before me as I run two, 6.5-mile loops.

It's very hard to watch people succeed when you're so far away from your own success. Then I remember: **When you compare, you despair.** So, I tell myself that God is showing me their success as a reminder that I can soon be enjoying the same triumph of completing this race. I keep pushing.

That competition taught me another secret: it gets easier when I stop worrying about the finish line.

"Just stay in this moment," I tell myself.

I persevere. And I finish!

I participated in my first triathlon in the Half Ironman competition in Augusta, Georgia, in 2014. It required running, biking, and swimming 70.3 miles. I'm swimming with my guide, Scott Johnson, who competes in races alongside me to make sure I'm okay. I have since competed in several more triathlons. Photo Credit: Joseph Kelley.

My performance was featured in video excerpts during the Concert for Valor attended by 100,000 people on Veterans Day, November 11, 2014, on the National Mall in Washington, DC. I attended with Khieda and the girls, and I was awed to watch a video that included former First Lady Michelle Obama telling the huge crowd that: "Cedric embodies the incredible resilience and strength of all of our wounded warriors."

She went on to describe how she had met me at the White House the previous year, and she cited me as an example of courageous soldiers who should be thanked and celebrated for our service. That was one amazing moment during an evening full of them at this event sponsored by HBO, Chase, and Starbucks. We watched performances by Bruce Springsteen, Rihanna, Eminem, The Black Keys, Zac Brown Band, Jennifer Hudson, Carrie Underwood, Metallica, Dave Grohl, and Jessie J. I loved watching the hosts, who included Jamie Foxx and George Lopez, and seeing the special tributes given by Oprah Winfrey, Will Smith, Steven Spielberg, Meryl Streep, and Reese Witherspoon. That evening was so special because I got to show everyone watching how to turn a breaking point into a Making Point.

Breaking at the New York City Marathon

In 2013, as I'm watching the New York City Marathon on TV, I declare, "Next year, I'm going to run that!"

On November 2, 2014, I find myself at the startling line as one of 50,869 runners in the city's biggest marathon ever.

I'm extra excited, because I just received a new pair of legs. They're a perfect fit! They're snug, but I don't think they'll be too tight for me to run.

Wrong! As we do short sprints to warm up at the starting line, something is not right. It feels like the prosthetic has a death grip on my leg. At the bottom tip of the leg, it feels like somebody is hitting me with a hammer.

Maybe it will get better...

We start running. I get to the top of the bridge. It still hurts.

We call Josh Kaufman, who's attending on behalf of Montel Williams, who wanted to come out and support me, but had another commitment. Josh brings me my walking legs. But they need adjustment.

"I need to find a wrench," I say.

Josh finds a firefighter who loans us a wrench. We adjust my legs, but one feels too tight, and the other is too loose. We keep making modifications. At Mile 6, I realize I must've stepped in a pothole. On top of that, we're getting blasted by 22-mile-per-hour winds. The gusts are so bad, that race officials actually started the hand cyclists three miles into the route, fearing they might get blown off the Verrazano Bridge.

Meanwhile, I'm still having mechanical problems. At Mile 8, my leg breaks in half! Screws pop out. Parts of my leg scatter on the street. I don't know how we can fix this!

I sit on the sidelines while my running guides go on a wild hunt for the parts we need to fix my legs. They dash in and out of pizzerias, hardware stores, tool stores, and bodegas, searching for screws and wrenches. They finally find the parts and reassemble the leg.

I've been sitting so long, I call my prosthetist, Mike Corcoran.

"Hold a cigarette lighter to it to mold it to your leg," he says. "Warm it, and push it closer to your leg, a little bit at a time. You won't be able to get it off, but it will get you to the end."

I do as I'm told, get up, and am able to keep running. It feels like the universe is throwing everything but the kitchen sink at me. That wind is worse than the hills of Boston! If I were in agony then, I don't even have a word to describe how I feel in New York.

It's nightmarish. I could easily climb onto the bus at Mile 16 and call it a night.

But I will not quit! I did not give up in Boston, and I will not do so in New York. Even though I have the best excuse in the world. What keeps me going is thinking about the story that would evolve:

Cedric: "Hey, I was running the New York Marathon and my prosthetic leg broke. I had to quit. I didn't finish."

Listener: "What? Your prosthetic broke? Hey man, I give you points for trying."

But I want to tell a better story.

Cedric: "Hey, I was running the New York Marathon and my prosthetic leg broke."

Listener: "What? And you finished the race anyway? In 10 hours? Wow, man, that's what I call perseverance! That's a miracle! If you can do that, you make me feel like I can do anything!"

As I push through the pain and keep running, I tell myself this:

Cedric, you're not going to be inspiring to others if you use the broken prosthetic to cop out. Having no legs, you stand out. Cameras and eyeballs gravitate to you. You have to represent as a winner, not a quitter. Even if others will let you off the hook, you cannot let yourself off the hook!

I decide that I'm going to tell how I won, despite what happened. I remember one of the greatest basketball games ever, when Detroit Pistons star Isaiah Thomas scored 45 points with a broken foot against the LA Lakers.

His strength was not physical. It was mental. And spiritual. So I kneel on a bridge and pray for God to bless me with the strength to keep going.

And that's where I'm drawing the strength to keep hobbling toward the finish line of the New York City Marathon as the sun sets, and I am one of only a few people straggling toward the end.

I will hunker down and outlast the storm. I'll have a smile on my face, a song in my heart, and a dance in my body, and in my feet. I will smile no matter what the weather.

I also feel that in doing this, I'm training for the marathon of life. A lot of people feel like they're *losing* the marathon of life. They feel stuck at Mile 17, staring up at a hill that looks impossible to climb. They're tempted to quit.

Here's where the mental toughness comes into play. Every time we refuse to give up, we build strength and a memory bank of endurance. We make a deposit in our personal strength account. Right now, as I'm struggling in New York, I make a withdrawal on the deposit I made during Boston when I persevered through the pain. The strength is liquid, cash, ready to spend immediately in the form of a jolt of confidence. I've done this before, and I can do it again, right now!

However, had I quit in Boston, it would be so easy to quit in New York. It all boils down to this question:

How long can you mentally endure punishment?

If you believe just a little longer, you kill the seeds of doubt. You get immediate relief when you keep believing. But if you allow yourself to quit in this moment, that becomes a place that you will revisit over and over and over again. You cannot and will not be able to escape the motivation to quit there.

On November 2, 2014, I ran the New York City Marathon. It was tough. Cold. Painful. I finished alongside a woman who had beaten cancer twice. Though we were among the last 10 people to finish out of the 50,000 who started the race, it was an exhilarating experience and yet another achievement that showed myself and the world that we are far more powerful than we believe.

But when you go back in your mind and remember, *I didn't quit in the pain that time, so I'm not going to quit now. And I will not feel sorry for myself. I will figure it out! I will persevere!*

Now, in New York, I did, even though I was among the last 10 people to finish the race. And it took me more than 10 hours! This, in comparison to the male winner, Kenyan Wilson Kipsang, who finished the marathon in two hours and 10 minutes.

Toward the end, I meet Gena Wilson, a cancer survivor from Glasgow, Scotland, who walked the entire marathon. We crossed the finish line together, and *Time* magazine published a photograph of us at the finish line in its November 6, 2014 edition.

We both persevered through the pain, and our photo became a blessing of inspiration to people around the world who saw that with faith, anything is possible, for anyone.

TRAINING FOR THE MARATHON OF LIFE

Since 2014, I have run the Boston Marathon three times, the New York Marathon once, the Disney Marathon three times, and I have done multiple half marathons, including a half Ironman. I also hiked the Boston Marathon once.

Meanwhile, I've built a great friendship with Boston bombing survivors Patrick Downes and Jessica Kensky. They have a beautiful love story about staying together after amputations and the trauma of the bombing.

"You should run this marathon," I told Patrick when we first met.

"No man," he said, "you're crazy."

"No, bro, you should do it," I said. "Think about what it would feel like to finish this marathon. Maybe I should run the Afghanistan marathon, where I got hurt, but they don't have one. But they do have a Boston Marathon, and you should run it."

"It's too far," Patrick said.

We probably had that conversation for a full year. One day, he said, "I'll hand-cycle it."

Patrick hand-cycled the marathon while I ran it for the second time. The following year, we both ran it. It was so emotional! Three years earlier, his leg was blown off, and now he's standing on the finish line, victorious!

We also participated in Red Sox games, thanks to the Achilles International's Freedom Team of Wounded Veterans. Patrick threw the opening pitch for the team the day before the marathon. And we were all there, cheering on the Red Sox and participating on the field in pre-game festivities along with nearly 38,000 fans in Fenway Park.

This is a moment where America gets it, I thought, *that freedom isn't free.* It costs something. And now all of these people are appreciative of the sacrifices we made.

I've also done the 48.6-mile Disney Marathon Series, which includes four runs in four days — a 5K, a 10K, a half marathon, and a full marathon. In 2016, I tackled that race with David Cordani, the CEO of the global health insurance corporation Cigna, which sponsored the event. *Runner's World* magazine published a feature story about us, and highlighted Achilles International for enabling us to participate.

In 2015, I ran the 48.6-mile Disney Marathon Series with David Cordani, CEO of the global health insurance corporation Cigna, which sponsored the event. We're celebrating at the finish line with Tyrrell Jamieson Schmidt.

HAND CYCLING: A WHOLE NEW FRONTIER

Joe Traum, director of the hand cycling program for Achilles, facilitated my participation in a marathon at Disney World in January of 2017 — using a racing chair. The problem? The chair arrived at my hotel in Florida just before the race. I had no time to train on it!

"The racing chair is what Cedric wants to do," says Joe, "so Achilles purchased it for him. I really wanted him to get a lot of training with the chair before he went out and did the half marathon, then the full marathon at Disney. But the time shift didn't work out very well because of the measurements for the racing chair. He did not get much training."

The story gets crazier, because I dive right into a full marathon! Organizers had to cancel the half marathon due to thunderstorms.

"I'm worried," Joe says.

"Don't worry about me," I say. "You know I can do it."

I'm confident, because I think hand cycling looks easy. I am so wrong! It is hard!

A déjà-vu feeling from Boston — that I'm embarking on a huge, difficult journey with no training — overwhelms me. Joe and others from Achilles run beside me for a little while, to make sure I'm okay.

"I saw pain in his eyes," Joe recalls. "His arms were hurting. He was sort of hitting a wall without hitting the wall. I was worried."

At the same time, all the people — other wounded veterans, our Achilles guides, and spectators — are yelling: "Keep going!"

"I'm going!" I push through the pain.

"You saw in his eyes that he was not going to quit," Joe says. "The way the muscles in his arms were moving announced that he wasn't stopping, either. That really was a wonderful moment to see him doing something completely other than what his normal is. He wasn't going to take no for an answer, and he accomplished the marathon."

I know I'm starting to sound like a broken record, but here's another example of pushing through terrible pain and receiving the blessing of accomplishment and serving as an inspiration to others to show that obstacles are made for us to obliterate.

Later, at the hotel, Kenya and I see Joe.

"Cedric doesn't stand around bragging that, 'I did it!'" Joe says. "He's very humble."

"I'm hurting," I tell Joe, who subsequently signs me up for cycling chair training camp so that I can compete with it in Boston and other marathons.

"He did the Disney race like a rock star," Joe says, "because with Cedric, there is no stopping. There is no, 'I can't.' For him, it's just another day."

Every year, I tell myself, I need to do something tougher. I need to push myself harder. I need to do something more challenging this year. You're either getting stronger, or you're getting weaker. Coasting, or hitting a plateau and staying there, are not options. Standing still is unacceptable. Never stop exerting effort. Every day you've got to be sharpening the sword. EVERY DAY!

How to Find the Power to Persevere Within Yourself

It may sound boring, but to find the power within yourself to persevere, you have to sit down and spend time by yourself. Get away from the noise for at least 10 minutes every day. No TV, no phones, no devices. No distractions. You can do this in your car when you drive alone. Just sit there before you go into the office.

Be quiet. Be still. And listen.

Delve deep inside yourself and get to know who you are on the inside. Not who you are in terms of your job title, or your family name, or your relationships, or where you went to school, or what you do on the weekend.

Find YOU.

The power to persevere is born out of knowledge of yourself.

Think of yourself as a jigsaw puzzle. You see your picture on the box. But inside are a thousand little pieces that all comprise the total picture of who you are. God made you in a perfect image; He knows what the picture is supposed to look like. And you know how hard it is to assemble the puzzle without the picture. Still, you have to study every little piece to figure out where it goes, and how it hooks together with all the other parts.

Do that with yourself. Ask: What are the most important aspects of my life? Why? What person or cause do I love so much that I would be willing to die for?

What are my spiritual beliefs? How can I strengthen them and use them every day to push myself harder, to persevere through pain and struggles, to receive the blessings that God has promised me?

What is my mission in life? What is the purpose that resulted in me being dealt this particular hand of cards, and how am I supposed to play them to help myself, my family, and the world?

What steps can I take today to begin executing that mission, even in the smallest ways?

What would I like for people to say about my life when they're eulogizing me at my funeral? Write a few sentences summarizing how people will describe your life, what you accomplished, and the legacy that you will leave. What can you do right now to make sure you achieve that?

Beat Down the Bullies: Fear, Pain, and Disbelief

I grew up being bullied. I never fought back, and the bullies just kept returning to torment me. As a kid, the bullies were two guys on the school bus. Then as I moved through life, the bullies kept showing up in the form of people and experiences.

Drill sergeants. The challenge of Ranger School. The Taliban. My injury. Pain. Fear. The pain and fatigue of marathons.

I realized, if you don't face down the bullies in second grade, sooner or later the bully will take the form of an Afghani soldier with an AK-47. You need to face that fear sooner or later, or it will grow bigger, more dangerous, and it will attack you.

When you finally find the courage to stand up to your tormenter, you will feel liberated. It may be scary and dangerous, but it's exhilarating. In fact, true living is being on the cusp of dying.

Life favors the person who is courageous. And when you do what scares you, the fear goes away. I've reached a point where I jump at fear immediately. I don't allow it to fester inside me and grow into something that holds me down.

One way to find courage is to think about the long-term consequences of allowing the bullies of fear, pain, and anxiety to stop you from living your best life. Where will that leave you in one year, five years, or on your deathbed? Which is worse, facing your fears and doing what scares you, or watching your life end without ever achieving your greatest dreams?

Write down your greatest goal in life. It could be anything, such as finding the perfect spouse, losing weight, building your dream home, having a baby, opening a business, earning a college degree, or opening a non-profit organization to help people.

Now write about what's holding you back from achieving that. What can you do to blast through those obstacles? Write out an action plan with weekly and annual goals that will help you build courage, and a history of successes, each serving as a step up toward achieving your goal.

I've learned that you don't have to figure out "how" things will work out. Put that in God's hands. Your job is to do what you can with what you have, and you will be amazed at the doors that God opens for you, when you pray fiercely and stay in complete faith.

Prayer has gotten me through every challenge in my life. God is listening, and responding 24 hours a day, seven days a week. Don't forget to ask for help. And don't be afraid to do so.

How to Boost Your Confidence

What can you do to boost your confidence by doing what may seem hard or even impossible right now? What steps can you take when you begin something and it becomes brutally difficult and you're tempted to give up? Write a list of your previous successes to remind yourself that you got through tough things before, and you can do it again.

The next step is easy: just do what you say you're going to do.

Start small. If you're trying to live a healthier lifestyle, promise yourself, "Today I'm going to get off the couch and take a walk for 10 minutes outside." Then do it.

If you want to lose weight, pledge to stop eating candy for a day. Stock up on fresh fruit for snacks, and stick to your plan. At the end of the day, pride in your accomplishment will inspire you to want to repeat that tomorrow. All you have to do is keep the momentum going, and add new goals: no junk food, a salad for dinner, more exercise.

You can also boost your confidence by finding power from the people who believe in you. A simple phone call from my wife during the worst moments of the Boston Marathon gave me the power to run four more miles to the finish line. She believed in me, so I believed in myself. Who is rooting for your success? When you're doubting your own ability to power through, try to imagine yourself through that person's point of view. You'll see that he or she thinks you can do anything, and *that* will trick you into believing that you can win!

Lastly, gratitude is your magic elixir to feel better, no matter how bad things get. When I'm in terrible pain, I force myself to make a mental list of how thankful I feel for my family, my life, my ability to travel the country as a motivational speaker, and so on.

Write a list of everything you're grateful for so you can dwell on that when you're experiencing pain. This will become your proverbial private jet that rescues you from your pity party and helps you soar into a new dimension that sparkles with blessings beyond belief.

_____

_____

_____

_____

_____

_____

_____

When I do this, God showers me with the biggest, most unexpected blessings. Meeting powerful people who provide experiences and opportunities that almost seem unbelievable. Providing media exposure to amplify my story in ways that inspire others. And putting me on new stages where I can show people that if Master Sergeant Cedric King can lose his legs on a battleground and then power through the pain to run marathons, then you can do anything in life that you desire.

5

Surviving: Choosing to Live

SURVIVAL IS YOUR SECRET WEAPON

When you're at your breaking point, you must choose to survive. While my injuries did not kill me, I had to make a conscious and constant choice to stay alive. Sadly, too many veterans who survive battlefield injuries lose their lives to the pain and anguish of the physical and emotional trauma they suffer afterward. This statistic is really hard to fathom, but it's real: 22 veterans kill themselves every day in the United States. That's according to a 2013 study by the US Department of Veterans Affairs.

That means, almost every hour, someone just like me gives up on life. Likewise, too many civilians succumb to suicide in the face of tough circumstances.

I understand this very well, because physical pain and depression once pushed me to the brink of death. During the months after my injury, I fantasized about taking my last breath, so my body would stop hurting. I imagined the relief of escaping the grief of losing my legs, and ending the frustration of adjusting to life without them.

But I refused to give up. I kept fighting for my life. And by the grace of God, I am here to tell you that **survival is a choice that you can make**. That's why I want to teach you some very basic, but critical, skills to help you survive anything.

The secret lies in the military acronym that soldiers use to triumph in life-or-death situations. It's called SURVIVAL. I'm about to break it down for you to use at any point in life when you feel stranded or shoved against a wall. A robbery, a health trauma, a job loss, a divorce, a death — we face countless scenarios every day that can become our breaking point.

Your breaking point is different from someone else's, because all obstacles are relative. One person's insurmountable pile of debt might be the same amount of money as another person's monthly mortgage that they pay with ease. A bout of pneumonia to a healthy person might be just as terrifying as a common cold to a person with a compromised immune system. Whatever is a crisis for you, you can defeat the obstacles, the enemy, the bully, even the brick wall, if you use the tenets of SURVIVAL along with two things: belief and action. Sometimes in the heat of a traumatic moment, it's hard to believe things will be different — especially in the face of zero evidence supporting improvement or change. So, when you lack belief, take action to embark on the path to survival. Here are the action steps for SURVIVAL:

S — Size up the situation

U — Use all your senses / Undue haste makes waste

R — Remember where you are

V — Vanquish fear and panic

I — Improvise

V — Value living

A — Act like the natives

L — Live by your wits, but for now, learn basic skills.

By God's grace, I **survived** the enemy's attempt to kill me with an IED. I returned to my *new* home at Walter Reed — greeted by my wife and my mom. They got me through those first weeks, then my daughters came, and their love for their dad was just as strong as ever. I didn't have my legs, but I could give them rides on my motorized scooter, and they loved that. They still loved me. Everybody still loved me.

Visitors who came to my room included family, friends, peers, and superiors from my entire Army career, to the Secretary of Defense, and the President of the United States. I had visits from strangers whose skill on their prosthetics gave me hope that I, too, would someday walk again on my own set of new legs. Inspirational people, loving relatives, and wounded warriors, like myself, who blended in with everybody else coming in and out of my room, encouraged me.

The support from doctors, nurses, hospital staff, driving instructors, occupational and physical therapists, volunteers, and countless others was unceasing and mind boggling. The facilities and the care and support given to Khieda and my family were incredible beyond words.

The Depth of My Anguish During those Early Months

Still, things are hard for me. During those first months, I pray a lot. My family prays for me. My friends and strangers pray for me. Everyone pours love and good wishes on me. I remind myself that I am extremely blessed.

> *I survived! I am healing! I am in the best facility possible to have the best outcome imaginable!*

Despite the positive energy coming at me from every direction, about six months after losing my legs, I feel hopeless. My depressed outlook coincides with two things. One is a very difficult choice that I made. The other is an uplifting, generous gift.

First, I make the choice to stop taking pain medication. Acutely aware that addiction to pain medication is a widespread problem among veterans, I wanted to avoid that path at all costs. The best way, I decided, was to stop taking meds altogether. So I did, determined to endure the pain without pills.

Second, Walter Reed sent Khieda, myself, and the girls on a ski trip with other veterans and their families to a resort in Vail, Colorado. The trip aimed to introduce us wounded warriors to new situations that would stimulate our minds during the healing process. We were supposed to have the time of our lives out there.

When we are at the beautiful resort, we're excited, because this is the King family's first ski experience. We even have the good fortune of our own ski instructor. So how am I going to ski without legs?

Skiing for me as a double amputee means sitting in a seat and going down the hill, tethered to our ski instructor. While I'm grateful for the experience, I don't feel challenged. Skiing that way is just not tough enough for me, and my heart is not singing the way it does when I run, which at this point in my recovery, I cannot do yet. In fact, I'm still learning how to walk on my prosthetics.

The most excruciating nerve pain — the worst I have ever felt — strikes. I feel hopeless that this pain will ever stop.

Outwardly, I am living the dream. I am with my family in a picturesque, snowy paradise; I'm having a truly first-time life experience; I'm watching my wife and kids learn to ski; we have the luxury of an attentive and skillful ski instruction so none of us gets hurt; and the trip is paid for. Who could ask for anything more?

But the pain consumes me. I can't imagine that it will ever ease — or end. Still, I refuse to take pain medication, because a life of addiction would be another form of hell. As a result, I am teetering on the edge of despair, two thoughts away from slipping down into an abyss and never escaping. I am not even 40 years old. How can I live the rest of my life like this?

I don't think I can…

We return to Bethesda, and things get even worse. I realize my entire life will be a series of doctors' appointments. I am in a constant battle against the pain. Even my desire to run seems daunting when the burning in my nerves screams out as I try to master walking on my new legs.

This is ridiculous. I'm stuck. I've got to live the rest of my life
with no legs.

I don't think I can get any lower. Here, as I contemplate suicide, my soldier's training in SURVIVAL saves my life, and it can save yours. Anytime, anywhere. Here it is, letter by letter:

S = Size Up the Situation

I size up my situation. I stepped on that bomb. I went into that room in that hut looking for evidence of bomb-making materials. I went to Afghanistan. I signed up for another four years. I became an Army Ranger. I joined the Army nearly two decades ago.

All that history could not be changed. All the decisions were mine, and I accepted responsibility for every one of them.

> *But… I have no legs. I am stuck in this hospital bed. I'd rather not be here.*

Anyone, not just veterans, can plunge into an abysmal place where life doesn't seem worth living. That is our breaking point, and that's where I found myself during that ski trip.

All I can do is implement my *go-to* move: prayer.

> *Lord, I can't figure it out right now. I need strength to get through the point of figuring it out. If you're not going to help me figure it out, that's fine: I just need strength. I don't need a boost of energy. I pray that you do not let me give up.*

U = Use All Your Senses / Undue Haste Makes Waste

The soldier's mind in an unknown territory snaps into assessment mode: What do I see? What do I hear? What can I touch? What do I smell? What, if anything, can I taste?

For me, in that hospital room, sight was my most powerful ability. I saw Khieda, my mom, and the girls. I never told them how I was feeling. Their hugs, their smiles, their love and compassion, and their presence saved me.

Here's another sense that's critical for survival: common sense. It countered the hopelessness that was stealing my will to live. Common sense reminded me that suicide only transfers your pain onto those who love you. The pain multiplies and magnifies when it touches other people. I could not, would not, consider "easing" my burden by throwing it onto them.

When someone takes his or her own life, they are deserting their problems and dumping them onto others, especially those closest to them. As painful as whatever you're going through may be, suicide is only a means to more pain. Most of the time people don't see that.

I learned from my prosthetist that a buddy of mine, a wounded vet, took his life recently. We're a small population of wounded vets. We know each other's pain. Every veteran who commits suicide sows more seeds of future hopelessness in those who come afterward.

Here's where another military acronym can help: SERE — Survival, Evasion, Resistance, Escape. As we utilize this survival formula, we are continuously *expecting support to come.*

My expectation for support came in the form of many people, including Stephanie Carter and her husband, Ash Carter, who was United States Deputy Secretary of Defense at the time.

"We made it our practice to go on the weekends to Walter Reed," recalls Mrs. Carter, who first visited when I'd been there for about two weeks. "We would just kind of see who we could, and bring cheer. We'd find out what happened, so we could better understand. We wanted to know if they feel like they had the equipment they needed. Often a wounded person would want to talk about what happened to someone who was familiar with where they'd just come from."

The Carters visited me often, met my family, and saw my Wall of Love. We got to know each other during these visits.

"Cedric always put on a brave face," Mrs. Carter says, "and was always trying to scan the environment for the most positive things he could pull out of it."

She observed me using all my senses! In addition to praying, I was trying to discover the good in my surroundings. I was going to survive. I was going to use my experience to uplift myself and others. Sharing moments of doubt is part of the healing process. Sharing is an active part of survival.

"Cedric's story is one of inspiration to show that one of the biggest determinants in life is not your intellect or talent," Mrs. Carter says, "but your resilience."

R = REMEMBER WHERE YOU ARE

In the military, when you come to the R in SURVIVAL, it's critically important to take account of where you are, so if you ever have to come back to that place, you will have a location of familiarity. If you know where you are right now, you can go elsewhere and come back.

In my case, I can always think of that hospital room for reference of where I was, and from where I rose. I was there.

Sometimes when you're in pain, disappointed, or scared, it's like being lost. Lost in frustration, lost in suffering, lost in heartache, lost in the letdown of yourself or others. You've got to figure a way back to the highway. You've got to find your way back to that spot you remember.

V = VANQUISH FEAR AND PANIC

Know that you will find no quick fix, no easy path, no magic spell to take you from utter hopelessness to your will to survive.

You might ask, *Where does this strength and will come from?*

It comes out of a place of desperation — a place where you're looking for the good because all you see are negativity and challenges. Sometimes our only place of refuge is in our thoughts. It takes looking straight into fear and executing in spite of that fear.

Tell yourself: *I will be mentally tough when things are not right in my life.* Just stay in the ring. Endure! Often, staying in the fight is just standing. It's not throwing punches; it's just weathering the storm. Sometimes you won't be able to out-score, out-fight, or out-kick the enemy, but you can outlast the enemy. Every one of us has enough strength to outlast the enemy, whether it takes the form of fatigue, frustration, lack of confidence, or any troublesome matter in your life.

Outlasting the enemy that's causing the fear and panic is outlasting your inner critic. Our real enemy is on the inside. Our inner critic comes in the form of our negative thoughts. It says, *Hey, look, I can't do this anymore.*

You can tell your inner critic: *I'm not going to quit. I'm going to allow the storm to pass by. I'm going to hunker down and endure. I'm going to stay on my post until the enemy tires and moves on. I don't know how long that's going to take, but I know I can man this post. I'm going to sing songs, keep a step in my dance, and do my best to keep a smile on my face — until the difficulty passes.*

When you outlast your inner critic, you are vanquishing fear and panic. But know this: another storm will come in a different form and your inner critic will be right back in your ears saying: *You can't!* Every time you make a choice to survive, just smile at your inner critic, your enemy, and commit to outlasting the storm, whatever form the storm may take.

I = IMPROVISE

If you're in the military and you're stranded, you have to improvise — use what you have. If you have no shoes, protect your feet with leaves; if you need string, use wire or vines; use wood for blankets. Be creative; you can always use something you already have in place of what you need or want.

You'll be most innovative if you stay calm. A state of panic will blind you to the resources in front of you. Also, you don't talk; you *do*.

Know, too, that failure is not final unless you believe it is. Instead, believe that failure is a prerequisite to an accomplishment. Just try as many times as humanly possible.

Unfortunately, we set caps and limitations on how many attempts we give ourselves before we quit. The truth is: we get unlimited attempts!

How am I going to make shoes out of leaves? I should be able to do it on the first try! My feet are cold! If you want it badly enough, you have to invest the time, trying again and again until you master it.

V = VALUE LIVING

To survive, you must value living. Gratitude enables me to do this, and it helps me persevere through the pain of my lowest moments at Walter Reed.

Every morning, I praise God for everything I can possibly feel grateful about: *Thank you for another day, Lord. Thank you for this day. Thank you for my eyes blinking; my ears hearing; another successful surgery; not getting an infection; in the realm of possible setbacks, thank you for those you've given me and those I didn't get. Thank you for keeping me healthy; thank you for the ability to put smiles on others' faces; thank you for these three meals a day.*

We can order whatever food we want from the cafeteria at Walter

Reed. We can ask for as much as we want. The same gentleman who drops off my food looks like and reminds me of my dad. We laugh a lot and have great conversations. I am thankful to see him every time he comes into my room.

During this time, I take my gratitude exercise to extremes, because it forces my mind to dwell in the positive, at a time when languishing in the negative threatens to prove deadly. So I thank God for the silliest little things: *Thank you for allowing the napkin to be dry; for them having red Gatorade; thank you for my pancakes being right today; thank you for these pancakes, this bacon, and this mug of butter.*

You can easily plunge to a place where your circumstances rob you of appreciation for your life. You've got to look at the smallest things, give thanks, and you will see that they are not so small after all.

About a month before my injury, the chaplain brought around Victor Frankl's book *Man's Search for Meaning.* When he was 39, the Austrian neurologist and psychiatrist was imprisoned in a concentration camp in Nazi Germany. At one point in the book, he writes of reaching into the watery soup they were fed, and every now and then, he'd find a pea at the bottom of his bowl. He wrote of how he would bring it up and feel so blessed just to have a pea. One pea!

Look around and find something as small as a pea. Give thanks for that small thing, and it will inevitably lead to gratitude for another thing, and another. Before long, this string of gratitude will help you survive because you are valuing living.

A = ACT LIKE THE NATIVES

Again, Dr. Frankl considered himself a survivor, not as the accomplished head of the department of neurology of Rothschild Hospital, which was his position before imprisonment.

I, too, have to consider that I am no longer Cedric on the battlefield; I am Cedric in the hospital. At first I try to hang on to my title, my rank, my definition of who I was and what I did up until the morning of July 25, 2012. All that is still part of me, but I have to act like — and understand — where I am in that moment.

Had I clung to the past, I would struggle and suffer from a deadly mix of who I was before versus who I am now. I have to accept: *this is where I am and this is who I am right now. This is what I have to work with.*

If you read or listen to Nelson Mandela's *Long Walk to Freedom*, you learn that during his 27 years on Robben Island and in Pollsmoor Prison, as he faced a life sentence of living in vicious conditions, he continued to find small glimpses of hope for freedom, even while watching fellow inmates get killed.

I adopt Nelson Mandela's attitude: if he could believe that one day he would be free from his life sentence of hard labor in a quarry, then I will never stop believing that my pain is not going to last forever. If I can handle my current circumstances, then I can believe that tomorrow will be a better day.

L = Live by Your Wits, But for Now, Learn Basic Skills

"Live by your wits" means live in this moment. In his book, *The Power of Now: A Guide to Spiritual Enlightenment*, writer and public speaker Eckhart Tolle stresses the importance of living in the moment. He believes that we hinder ourselves when we dwell on the past and the future, which causes us to miss the magic of the present moment.

"Live by your wits, but for now learn basic skills" means live as if this is the only moment that ever exists. Prior moments are gone;

future moments don't exist yet. If a soldier is stranded in a life-or-death situation, we acknowledge basic skills as facts. The internal dialogue might go like this: *I have the ability to shoot. I can talk on the radio. I can apply first aid.*

That know-how confirms that I will live in that moment. Soldiers caught in these survival situations live by the knowledge of their basic skills. That helps them get to a better place until the storm subsides.

Lay a Foundation for Survival

If you're feeling despair, fight through the pain. You will find your strength. Fight through your breaking point, and you will find your Making Point. Create a *go to* move long before you get deep in the hole. Your *go-to* move may be the thing that saves you. It could be praying, journaling, meditating, calling a certain person who's always there to help, or taking a run to help you burn off anger and calm down.

Establish your life-saving plan now, before you sit in that car contemplating pulling the trigger. If you proceed, know that everybody who loves you and everybody who has good feelings toward you will absorb your pain exponentially.

This hopelessness and the repercussions of suicide apply to anyone in that moment of despair. The question of how to survive *in that moment* can only be answered by you. You have to acknowledge that, and fight forward to your answer.

God knows how much I can bear. Your higher power knows how much pain it takes before it's going to kill you. How much it will take to destroy you — for you to ultimately quit and give up. But He knows what it takes to fight back. He can't give you too much — just enough — to get the best out of you.

God needs the hopelessness to be conjured up — if He doesn't put enough of the poison in you, you'll never build up immunity. Your higher power also knows how much it will take to build you. When you get a flu shot, you get just enough of the virus to find out how much of a fighter you are.

This might seem easier said than done. How did I do it? How can you do it?

Lay a foundation for survival so you can implement SURVIVAL in those desperate situations and moments. I was born into a family that prayed; prayer and worship are a huge part of Khieda's and my parenting philosophies. Favorite psalms were passed down through my family, so I can easily say prayer is my go-to move. Prayer encompasses both belief and action for me.

> *But, Cedric, what if I didn't grow up with God or some other higher power? What can I do?*

On top of my very prayerful foundation is an immense layer of personal development that has been fundamental in my belief that burdens and obstacles are actually blessings.

About six years before my injury, I got into reading self-help books. I read Dr. Joseph Murphy's book, *The Power of Your Subconscious Mind*. At the time, I had a friend going through chemo, and I shared with her what I was learning from the book. I told her, *Your thoughts are things. Everything started as thoughts: cars, airplanes.*

Around the same time, my uncle George, my dad's brother, was visiting, and we discovered a mutual interest in motivational books.

"Darren Hardy's *The Compound Effect* launched it for me," Uncle George recalls. "I said to Cedric, 'You've read this one before?'"

We shared books, often telling each other, "You really have to read this one."

My journey into this layer of higher thinking started when my friend Kenya sent me a CD by the late entrepreneur, author, and motivational speaker Jim Rhon. My response? *This is amazing!* I'd never heard anything like it. Yet it was comforting and familiar, because it reminded me of Sunday school and something my mom would listen to. So I asked, *What else is out there like this?*

Before I knew it, I had surrounded myself with books on personal development, motivational sermons, and a higher vibration of thinking. Those felt right, like the perfect complement to all I'd been taught through religion.

I started reading everything I could find: Les Brown, Dr. Wayne Dyer, Napoleon Hill.

In hindsight, God was sparking this curiosity and hunger for self-development to prepare me for the morning of July 25, 2012, when my catastrophic injury would require a huge amount of understanding on how to overcome obstacles, remain positive, and survive.

By then, I had a storehouse — a cache of ammo — to battle negativity. Between my prayers and my motivational, personal development, as well as philosophical studies, I had a ready-to-fire, endless surplus of positive thoughts. With these books, I had built a foundation for survival.

BRAINWASH YOURSELF INTO SUCCEEDING AT SURVIVAL

I've brainwashed myself. Now, I don't know any other way to think. Every single day I spent on personal development, the muscle memory in my mind was preparing me for that moment.

That moment was the test. All that study, all those sermons, all that Sunday school with my mom as my teacher, and all that reading and listening to amazing thought leaders, prepared me for that moment in my life.

But the test went beyond that moment. That moment represents the beginning of the biggest obstacle of my life. The test continues today. The test came in the form of the doctor telling me my expectations were too high if I wanted to run within a year of losing my legs; in the form of re-learning to drive and feel independent again; in the form of dealing with the phantom pains in feet I no longer have; in the form of the very real nerve pain in the legs I still have; in the form of being visited by dignitaries in the hospital.

This way of thinking — on top of my Christian upbringing, my Army training, and my personal development conditioning — has become something that materializes real results.

So, when I'm sitting in the hospital bed and people are coming and staying for hours in my room that looks like a museum with my Khieda-created wallpaper of happiness and hope and love, life is preparing me for everything in this moment and beyond.

The *moment* I stepped on that IED knew I needed armor on me; the armor was a lifetime of devoted prayer and the wisdom of others who made connections between thoughts and outcomes. All of it conspired to teach me to believe in things despite having no evidence.

Everything conspired to say: you're going to walk through this moment of losing your legs, and you're going to do it in a way that inspires others to say, *I saw Cedric do THAT, so I can deal with my own situation with grace and courage.*

And the way I did that was with my mind.

Use the Bully to Defeat the Bully

When I first stood up on my new legs, the pain was immeasurable. My inner critic said, *If I can't take a step without pain, how am I going to run without pain?*

In that moment, the obstacle seemed huge! It always does when you first undertake anything. That's the bully saying, "You've got no business being here, and let me show you how hard it's going to be."

I know a thing or two about bullies. While my amazing mom was raising me to be a compassionate, caring young man, two older boys were tormenting me in elementary school.

Though my sister-cousin Jennifer was on the bus with me, without an older brother or sister, we were basically prey for the older kids. They were really tough on me.

One kid would pick on me every day on the bus. I always stood up for myself, and if anyone picked on Jennifer, I would stand up for her, too. I was very protective of her, and if I heard her tell somebody to leave her alone or saw some boy pull her hair, I jumped right in, even though I was smaller and weaker than those older guys.

I sometimes got beaten up on the back of the bus by these stronger, bigger, older kids. But I was not *not* going to stand up for myself or Jennifer. Even then I knew that **trying meant not losing. And not losing meant winning.**

I didn't lose fights, and in some strange way, that equaled success. But I did lose emotionally. My spirit was beaten down; on the inside, I'd lost the fight before it even started because I told myself I couldn't win against such a big obstacle.

Those days of elementary school fights ended, but the bully evolved from those older kids on the bus, to an older kid in high school. Then the bully became the drill sergeant in the Army. Then it was my first boss in the Army. Then Ranger School became the bully. Then it was the Taliban. Finally, this injury became the bully.

I was afraid of what could happen: the problem was always the **fear** of the bully, not the bully. Once I became injured, any fear I had of becoming injured disappeared. I wanted to go back and tell young Cedric: "There is nothing you can do until you face the fear, not the bully. There is no bully after you."

We have to face our fears. We must do the thing we're afraid of doing. If you don't face that fear of the fourth grader, one day he's going to turn into an Afghani with an AK-47 pointed at you!

In combat, every single day you do a patrol. You get put in an environment where people are shooting at you. It's terrifying the first time, but if you continue to do it, it's almost addictive. You start to thrive on it! It's invigorating! You can get addicted to standing up to the thing that you fear. It's liberating to stand up to your fears.

If you talk to anybody who's been in a shoot-out several times — they will tell you that in the moment before anybody gets hurt or killed, it's a pure adrenaline rush. When you come out of it, if you lose a friend, or a body part, it is something that you will never forget. You're so close to dying, you think maybe that's what living truly is. That epiphany is totally exhilarating.

When the voice in your head is saying, "This is too tough; give up now," that's the bully telling you that you don't belong here. But you can't stay in a space where the bully is saying that you don't belong. By his presence — not by the difficulty — you know you belong here.

Recognize the voice of the bully and celebrate your awareness. Then you have the power to pursue what's in your heart: survival.

Oh my goodness, I may never do the things that my heart is say-ing I can do if I let the fear of the bully dominate my thoughts.

The enemy is there to help you become a better you. It's there to challenge you; it's your sparring partner.

No matter the bully or enemy or obstacle, it's there for you to become stronger. You have to understand that this person or thing has been put in your life to make things better, even though it may not look like it in the difficult moment.

You need a strong opponent to become good at any sport. You need a sparring partner to become the heavyweight champion of the world. You've got to learn how to bob, weave, jab — and you're not going to learn how to do that unless someone is coming at you. The one thing you can't do when your sparring partner gets in the ring: you can't bolt. If you bolt, the bully will find you in a new form and challenge you again, just the way he did for me.

What you have to know is this: what separates the people who broke in situations like those faced by Nelson Mandela and Victor Frankl, is that others didn't stay in the ring. Those who were not broken were fighting to survive with their ability to say, "Okay, I'm staying in the ring to battle this beast, and I'm going to figure out a strategy to win!" Life is a perpetual series of bouncing back — again and again — from adversity. Believe, again and again and again, that you are going to survive, even if you have no evidence!

BUILD AN ARSENAL OF SMALL WINS TO SURVIVE

We all need to have that part of us that says, *I've been down before, and I can come back. I need to be on the canvas every now and again. I was denied that time, but that doesn't mean I can be denied this time.*

So many people want to live life without failing. You'll succeed so much more if you have that loss on your record. If Muhammad Ali hadn't lost to Joe Frazier, he wouldn't have beaten George Foreman.

In order to survive, your response to failure must be: "I needed that failure."

I'm going to make you beat yourself with your own strength — you turn your opponent's strength into your ally so you can overcome obstacles.

Have you ever seen a football team use its defense to beat the other team's offense or vice versa? This is how your bully should be used. This is how your failures should be used.

Look at every obstacle as an opportunity. Every person, every denial, every rejection — they're all there designing a better version of you. You have to look at things that way. Every single tear, every single pain, every mountain in front of you is there to strengthen you. So many people would argue and say some problem or issue they're facing is systemic in their community. They'll say, "It's not me; it's the system," or they'll blame the adversity on their credit, their family name, their boyfriend or girlfriend. They're giving that adversity the power to derail them by not accepting it.

We all have to take responsibility and own it. We can't shuck it away. We can not only take credit for the good, but we must take credit for the bad.

Remember, there is no reward in small belief. I would rather die believing than live doubting. It's the easiest of the two circumstances — even if believing is so far-fetched due to lack of evidence.

There is, however, reward in slaying small giants. If you're not the person who's won, you can start right now by conquering the small giants.

You can go to the gym when you don't feel like it. That is a win. You're going to feel like you just slayed a small giant, because you overcame the inner critic and got off the couch when you didn't feel like it. You slayed the bully inside: your inner critic.

Cross the room and go to talk to the pretty girl when you think you don't have a shot. Get up and do it anyway. Be okay with looking stupid; be confident enough to try. Even if you do get shot down, you did the tough part. That is a win!

If you're trying to lose weight, eat well for one meal. When you get to your next meal, you will have the win of a single, well-eaten meal on your mind.

We are surrounded all day, every day with small obstacles. If we consciously choose to face and conquer those little things, when we are faced with a medium-sized obstacle, we can look to our small successes, and confidently try to slay medium giants.

When you do this, you feel great about yourself, and you build up a cache. Next thing you know, you have the confidence to try slaying huge, inconceivable giants. But you won't always succeed. You need your butt to get kicked in such a way that you can look back over your life, and say, "I've been here before. I made it out of that; I can make it through this."

When we take a detour around the obstacle, we've cheated ourselves out of a mentality that could have helped us sail through that obstacle and the next. We don't have that perspective. Taking a detour can stunt your personal growth and your survival.

As you slay giants, think of gumbo — turning scraps into something beautiful and tasty. Some of the best gains in history came because somebody got injured or faced an obstacle.

USE GRATITUDE TO SURVIVE

Prayer and personal development helped me change my attitude. They changed the way I feel about the pain. Instead of focusing on the pain and when it will end, I tell myself that for every bad, there is an equal or better blessing that comes with that pain.

If you are living what feels like a depressed, downtrodden life, focus on the things you can change — or you're going to continue living your life in that low spot. What I chose to do: I can't change the fact that I have no legs. If I focus on that too long, I'll always be in that moment.

What I can change is my thought pattern. Early on, I focused on the legs I'd get. I focused on the challenge of using them. I focused on the blades I'd get for running. I focused on the challenge of using those blades so I could push myself to move fast again.

Having pain every single day, thinking, *This will never change,* would be to waste moments focusing on something I had no control of. So I use my go-to prayers. **I speak or think statements of gratitude. I morph my thoughts into what I can change. I act and I believe in whatever ratio of acting and believing it takes to get me through the obstacle.**

> *Lord, I need you so bad. There's nothing I can do about how bad this pain is. Help me see what's going right. I've got my family. My daughters are healthy. We can laugh together.*

Giving thanks for even the simplest things, such as a dry napkin in the hospital, shifts my thoughts away from the pain, and I'm still focusing on the moment. And in that moment, it changes from living in pain to living in gratitude.

Know this: you can minimize the thing that you're struggling with by using your thoughts of gratitude. Each time you do this, you start to form a habit.

Gratitude can get you back to the highway. It will direct you onto the right road to reach your destination: survival. From there, you can find your destiny: to use your survival to create something meaningful for yourself and others.

SURVIVAL 101: BUILDING YOUR PERSONAL TOOL KIT

Just as you should have a first-aid kit in your car, along with jumper cables, and a spare tire, you should carry this Personal Survival Tool Kit in your mind at all times. Right now I'm going to help you build it.

Write out your responses to each point on your phone, in a notebook, on your computer, or on the spaces provided below.

GOD. What higher power can you call upon during your darkest moments? What is your relationship with God? How can you deepen this connection and cultivate stronger faith that God will provide strength to survive during your most difficult moments?

_____

_____

_____

_____

PRAYER. What is your favorite scripture? What are your favorite prayers that give you strength to overcome pain, depression, and fear? Write them here.

_____

_____

_____

_____

A MANTRA. Write a personal mantra that expresses you as your most powerful self. It can be as simple as, "I am strong" or "I will survive" or "God is always carrying me."

_____

_____

_____

_____

PEOPLE WHO LOVE YOU. Make a list of the people who love you unconditionally. How would your choice not to survive affect them?

_____

_____

_____

_____

YOUR IMPACT ON COMMUNITY. Consider how your friends, family, colleagues, and community would feel if you chose not to survive. Would their pain be a fair exchange for ending your pain?

_____

_____

_____

_____

PEOPLE & PLACES THAT CAN HELP YOU. What resources can provide you with the therapy, medication, housing, employment, transportation, recreation, or training that you need to rise up and out of your current situation?

_____

_____

_____

_____

ACTION. What new activities can you do   such as meditation, yoga, prayer, socializing, physical activity — that can help you take control of your life, enjoy yourself, and thrive?

_____

_____

_____

_____

PAST VICTORIES. List experiences when you have triumphed over tragedy, trauma, and everyday problems. Keep the list handy to remind yourself that you've made it through big problems in the past, and you have the strength to do so now.

_____

_____

_____

_____

WHO & WHAT I'M LIVING FOR. I live for God, my family, and all the people I can help every day. I also live for the life mission to use my injury as a lesson to others that we all have the power to persevere, no matter what. So, who are you living for? What cause are you living for?

_____

_____

_____

_____

6

Celebrating Life and Love

July 25, 2013 — My First Alive Day

"No, no, no! You could hurt yourself!"

That's what my family is telling me — because I want to climb a mountain.

It's my first Alive Day — the one-year anniversary of surviving the explosion in Afghanistan — and about 60 of us are gathering to celebrate near my Aunt Karen and Uncle Mac's place in Georgia. We're here because Khieda said she wanted to do something super-special for my first Alive Day to rejoice that I am not only alive, but thriving — with new legs. So, my heart leapt at the opportunity to travel here and enjoy time with my family and friends. Later, we're going to have a cookout with lots of music and family fun. But right now, I want to celebrate by conquering a physical challenge:

I'm going to climb Stone Mountain.

Stone Mountain, if you've never heard of it, is the Mount Rushmore of the South, with carvings of Jefferson Davis, General Robert E. Lee, and Lt. General Thomas "Stonewall" Jackson. Stone

Mountain Park near Atlanta hosts festivals, camping, and events like weddings and family reunions. The "mountain" itself, a massive outcrop of quartz-type rock, is 825 feet high and covers almost 600 acres.

As an Army Ranger, I've had my run-ins with mountains, and I always survived. Those times, I didn't have a choice; the mountains were something I had to survive as part of training or deployments. This time, I'm choosing to go to the mountain. It has a powerful meaning; it symbolizes the huge obstacle that God has placed on my life's path. Climbing this mountain will demonstrate my ability to overcome anything. It's a test of faith, of believing that we have the power to do anything when we believe in ourselves and when we believe in God. I learned this as a kid in Sunday school, in Mark 11:23: "For verily I say unto you, That whosoever shall say unto this mountain, be thou removed, and be thou cast into the sea; and shall not doubt in his heart, but shall believe that those things which he saith shall come to pass; he shall have whatsoever he saith."

I believe, I have faith, and I know that my mountain-sized obstacle can be cast into the sea, which is just another way of saying: gone. But my family is worried about the danger of climbing with prosthetics. Worry is all over the faces of my cousins, aunts, and uncles.

"What are you gonna do when the boulders come up?" they ask. "What are you gonna do if you fall down?"

I smile and chuckle warmly at them. "I just got blown up by a bomb. I'm pretty sure me falling down on a boulder isn't gonna do me any harm."

These are the people who love me the most, and I know their intention is not for me to hold myself back, but to keep myself safe and protected. Their concern is an expression of love — as it was when they said, "Don't do Ranger School," and "Don't run marathons."

Then, as now, my heart is overruling their caution and telling me I have to follow through.

So now that we're standing at the foot of the mountain, I'm staring up at the giant boulders, plants, and trees. It's steep. It's rugged. And it's the personification of me overcoming this tough place in my life.

"I have to do this," I declare.

"If you're going to do it," Khieda says, "I'll be with you."

Other family members join us, and we start climbing the mountain. Khieda rips off a tree branch, hands it to me, and says, "Here, hold onto this." Our slow ascent takes us past a sign warning, "Proper footwear required (non-slip sole)" and "Do not attempt" if you have a medical condition. The slope is gradual at first, but we are not walking on dirt or cement. We are walking on stone that's as slippery as a wet kitchen countertop! Then come the moss-covered boulders. As I do my best to stay upright with my stick, my mind flashes back to my worried relatives' faces.

Man, this is everything I thought it would be!

These boulders are getting bigger, the Georgia sun is blazing, and I'm struggling. So, I concentrate mostly on not falling, and I keep pushing forward, sometimes on all fours. About halfway up, I remember how a few days before this, I had declared at church: "I think I'm gonna climb Stone Mountain." Then all of a sudden on the mountain, we see a lady from church.

She is overjoyed, and exclaims: "You said you were gonna climb Stone Mountain!" Seeing her there was a reminder that we have to *believe* in what we say, so we can *create* what we say.

By now, a little crowd is going up with us, and it's starting to get steep. I don't know how I'm going to continue. I'm on all fours, and barely making it! I'm taking one step at a time, doing whatever I can with my arms, my hands, my legs. My knees, both my real one and my prosthetic one, are buckling from the awkward angles required to traverse the boulders.

My family had warned: "It's gonna get really steep."

To me, it's always been steep. My mindset is already on a different level. Right now, I'm in "overcome" mode, and not just when it gets steep, but from the beginning. If it's steep now and it's gonna get steeper, that's the gear I'm already in. Keep a positive perception of the obstacle. Stay in that mindset that it's tough now and the degrees of difficulty can increase with bigger boulders, a greater elevation grade, hotter heat, a more blinding sun. Those are all metaphors for life, when you're climbing your personal mountains, determined to make it to the top.

As I'm climbing, I consider only one option: reaching the top. No matter how steep or dicey it gets, I'm in the moment, working hard to overcome the toughest thing in my life: the mountain. In Ranger School, I first viewed the mountain as my opponent. But when I changed my perception to see it as a friendly ally, it transformed into a sparring partner to push me in ways that having my feet on safe, flat ground could not.

We all have to do that. We all *can* do that with our obstacles. We turn the obstacle into something that helps us. I'd already started to prove this to myself, by running a 5K a few months before my Alive Day. Getting to the top of this mountain can't be tougher than that.

So, you have to put yourself in challenging situations. A version of yourself in the future will benefit from looking back at the challenges you're tackling today, just as the Cedric scrambling up slippery, steep Stone Mountain can look back on the success of conquering mountains in Ranger School. That experience is telling me that *I can do this, here and now!*

And I finally do it. I reach the top of Stone Mountain — intact — on my first Alive Day! The view is incredible, so we all start taking pictures. Then I tell our group, "I want to go back down."

"No!" everybody says in unison.

One year after the bombing, my extended family celebrated my "Alive Day" with a barbecue and a climb up Stone Mountain in Georgia. Climbing the mountain a year after losing my legs showed myself and the world that anything is possible when we persevere through pain and obstacles.

I want to walk, crawl, and scramble down, the same way we came up. But my family wants to get back to the party and have some barbecue, so we all take the gondola back down. My relatives who had looked so worried are thrilled to see me coming down safely, and they're proud that I succeeded.

I cast my mountain-sized obstacle into the sea, just one year after losing my legs. Climbing Stone Mountain boosted my confidence.

Plus, it showed everyone around me — including the strangers climbing the mountain around us — that anything is possible. And it gave my family one more thing to celebrate on my Alive Day.

It All Starts Deep Inside You

The message in this chapter is all about cherishing the love and support in your life, and creating it if you don't have it. The most important thing for you to understand right now is that it all starts deep inside you. It's like you have to calibrate an imaginary magnet inside yourself, and turn it on full power, and it will attract everything you need. It starts in your mind, and gives you ideas to take action. Then you have to find courage in your heart to implement whatever ideas are coming to you. I'm about to explain how this works.

After my injury, I calibrated my internal magnet to attract opportunities to make myself stronger and prove that I can overcome the obstacle of losing my legs. That inspired my family to organize my Alive Day celebration. And it presented the opportunity to climb Stone Mountain. I had to give effort before I could receive the confidence to push on toward even bigger obstacles. Francis of Assisi once said, "For it is in giving that we receive." Every religion in the world says you reap what you sow in some form or another. When you sow good seeds that help people, you're rewarded with an endless harvest of the sweetest fruits.

All my life, my family has been supporting me by planting seeds of love, character, strong personal values, perseverance, and mental toughness in me. As I grew, these seeds sprouted and made me into the person I am today. Now it's my responsibility to keep receiving love and support, to continue planting seeds of faith and hope and confidence within myself, and very importantly, to help other people. Love and support, giving and receiving, are all one big, endless circle that can keep getting bigger and stronger when you follow my action steps.

Build Your Own Support Network

God blessed me by putting me in the middle of all these kind, loving, supportive people. Our family is huge on both my mom's and my dad's sides. I have 40 first cousins. I have an aunt who is one of 19 children! I count my blessings and thank God for my family every day. Not everybody is born into such a such a close-knit family. Some people who are reading these words have no family. No friends. No support system.

When you're going through tough times, that's when you need support most. Sometimes we have a support system, but as soon as trouble comes, they're gone. Those aren't real friends. Sometimes when we're suffering or facing major challenges, we push people away. We don't want them to see us in that condition, or we feel ashamed, or unworthy of the kindness they're trying to share. And sometimes we won't admit that we need help.

Soldiers are tough. We're survivors. We're self-sufficient. But we also operate in platoons, and we know we've all got each other's backs in treacherous situations. We all know that no matter how tough we are as individuals, our lives depend on each other. Life is the same way.

Support Is A Two-Way Street

Support is a two-way street. First you have to get on the road to believing that support is important. Then take a step toward what you need, and believe that this journey will lead you to the support that you need. The best place to start is online.

If you have a health condition, an addiction, marital problems, financial struggles, any problem you can name, know that you are not alone. Someone else needs that same help right now. So go online and find a support group, a chat room, testimonial videos, a Facebook group, or a phone conference line. If you can't find help online, call the library, your church, the community center, or the local hospital, and ask for assistance in finding your group. You may even want to completely immerse in that field by applying for a job or volunteering with the organization that can help you.

Just taking the step to find support is the start. Then think of a mantra, like I did when I saw Oscar Pistorius running two weeks after I lost my legs: *I'm going to be running 10 miles next year.* Remember, that was my mantra when I had no legs! I wasn't even close to getting prosthetics to walk, much less run. But I declared it, I believed it, and I got the support to make it happen. So, your mantra could be:

> *I'm going to find a support system this year. I'm going to find a support system that helps me get better.*

If you are at your breaking point, and are sorely missing the support of others, take that first step, believing, trusting, and knowing that the support will come. Belief plus action equals results.

WHAT IF YOUR SUPPORT WANTS TO HOLD YOU BACK?

Here's another scenario: what if your support system is broken?

My family didn't want me to climb Stone Mountain on my Alive Day. They wanted me to stay safe and keep my feet on the ground, not scrambling up those slippery boulders or teetering up that steep incline. They almost lost me once, and now they wanted to keep me out of harm's way.

But, wait! I want to do this!

Often when we have a dream, whether it's opening a business, running a marathon, changing jobs, or moving to a new city, we have to be careful with that dream. We have to protect it, and share it with those who will also protect it and support it.

When I said, *I'm going to be running 10 miles next year*, the doctor told me that may have been too ambitious. I knew the force of my desire in my heart was strong, but I could have very easily slouched back on my hospital bed and said, "Yeah, you're right."

We have to know that there's a balance between what our heart pushes us toward, and what we take action toward, in spite of having no evidence in the physical world, which includes what our doctors, loved ones, bank balances, enemies, and fears are telling us.

You're right. I shouldn't climb Stone Mountain. I shouldn't run this marathon; I should let the cart take me to the finish line.

For me, that's a big, No!

Support is a two-way street: you have to be willing to accept it when it's given, and give it back.

If your heart is telling you to quit your day job and start your own business, but your family is saying, "Don't do that! It's too risky!" look for organizations that help people with ideas for a business. You are not the first to desire to get from the mediocrity of point A to the heart-leaping dreams of point B. Create that vision board. Find business support. Strike up conversations with small business owners, network with entrepreneurs, and empower yourself with knowledge so your dream can become a reality.

If your support system is telling you not to pursue your dreams, ask yourself: *Is this person saying I can't accomplish my dream? Or are they saying if they were in my shoes, they don't think they could?* Don't let others project their limitations on your infinite possibilities! Decide for yourself that you can do it! That you can do anything!

For those of you who don't have support: don't wait for support to find you. Go forward and your greatest allies will come once you've made up your mind to accomplish something. You find people on the way.

Sometimes we fool ourselves into thinking things should be lined up before we start. "Oh, I'd go to the gym if I had a workout buddy. I have no workout buddy, so I won't go to the gym." Try something different: go to the gym with the intention of finding a workout buddy, and commit to staying in the game until that workout buddy comes. Tell the trainers at the gym or the front desk staff that you're looking for a workout buddy. Take action. Get creative.

Start where you are. Life tends to say, "I'm going to give you one friend, then two friends — only after you've made the decision to say, 'I want friends.'"

HOLD ON FOR DEAR LIFE TO YOUR SUPPORT

It's date night for me and Khieda, and we're at a concert. R&B stars Keith Sweat and Mint Condition are performing. Our seats are close to the stage and we're having a good time, so when Keith asks all the married couples to raise their hands, ours go up. I'm super comfortable; my prosthetics are off, enjoying a nice night out with Khieda. The girls are safe at home. Can it get any better?

Next thing I know, he's calling us up on stage in front of thousands of people. It's crazy; I want to tell him I don't have legs, and I want him to say, "Don't worry about it, man!" I want him to give me a pass because I have no legs.

But another voice inside is saying, *Put your legs on and go up like everybody else!*

So, I put on my legs — I'm wearing jeans — and I'm thinking, *I can't miss a step!* My inner critic, who wanted to take a pass on this opportunity, is saying, "Show him your legs; let him know you might fall."

That's a cop-out, man!

Khieda looks excited; she believes in me and knows I would love the experience of dancing with her on stage at a live concert as Keith Sweat blows one of his love ballads. She's holding my hand, smiling, and leading me up on stage. But the whole time, I'm thinking about how my walk doesn't look like everybody else's, and there is a part of me inside that's reassuring myself: *It doesn't matter, even if you fall down, you make an idiot of yourself — you still are the winner because you challenged the inner critic and got out of your seat.*

So, we get on the stage and I'm holding on to Khieda for dear life as we're slow-dancing in front of the musicians. I'm just rocking back and forth, doing my best to keep my balance, and I'm tipping over, and she's holding me up, and here we are acting like I didn't have two amputations. We're just one of several couples on the stage while Keith Sweat serenades us and the crowd.

The best part? We had the time of our lives that night! What started out as a date night, as in all of life, turned into so much more. I was faced with an opportunity to overcome my inner critic, who likes to remind me that the rest of the world would be okay if I give excuses. Everybody would be fine if I had said, "Hey, Keith Sweat and Mint Condition, thanks for inviting me and the love of my life up on stage to dance, but I've got these prosthetics, and it would be awkward for all of us if I fell. So, I'm gonna pass."

I didn't succumb to the inner critic. I fended it off with the courage to accept that I'm different, that I have a unique way of walking and slow dancing, and that all of these traits make me the one and only Cedric King. It's up to you to view yourself that way as well.

That night also gave Khieda the opportunity to be my support, literally. I know she can't support me unless I'm willing to be supported. Had I not found the courage to go on stage with her, I would have robbed her of the chance to support me.

Dorothy did not find the Scarecrow, the Tin Man, and the Cowardly Lion until she got on the yellow brick road. She wanted Glenda the Good Witch to go with her, but Glenda disappeared. We want assurances before we get on the yellow brick road, whatever that yellow brick road may be, but we have to start walking on our own — and take that first step — before we are blessed with our partners.

Just Be Dad

I'm in the car with my daughters, and Amari says she's having a tough time making friends at school.

"Hey, listen," I say. "You've got to apply effort in school or in meeting new friends. You can't just sit by and wait for good things to happen to you."

I launch into a metaphor about how I had to exert a huge effort to learn to walk again, run marathons, and do triathlons. I didn't accomplish any of those things without putting in a huge effort. Since I lost something visible and literal — my legs — my daughters understand my point.

"Oh, I remember," says Amari, who's 12 at the time. "Okay, Dad, I got you."

She understands the lesson.

Losing my legs has given me the opportunity to use the experience to learn, grow through it, and then to teach it again. Teaching is learning twice.

My daughters want me to just be dad. It doesn't matter to them that I have no legs.

THE PIED PIPER OF THE NEIGHBORHOOD

I didn't understand it at the time, but I have been practicing the spiritual principle of giving and receiving since I was a little kid. It's always been in my heart to help anyone who needed it, including the neighborhood bullies! Little did I know, I was planting seeds that would grow a powerful crop of blessings later in life.

As a little boy growing up in a trailer in North Carolina, I remembered learning in Sunday school that "God loves a cheerful giver." It's in 2 Corinthians 9:6-7. The rest of it says, "The point is this: whoever sows sparingly will also reap sparingly, and whoever sows bountifully will also reap bountifully. Each one must give as he has decided in his heart, not reluctantly or under compulsion, for God loves a cheerful giver."

But what motivated me to help other kids was simply that I wanted to.

"Cedric was a child who would give away the last crumb of food in our house if he thought someone was hungry," my mom remembers.

One time, my mom was making hot dogs, and I asked her to share with my friend Quentin.

"Cedric, this is all we have," she said.

"But Ma, he's hungry. Quentin needs to eat, Ma."

My mother, Sandra Williams, raised me with the help of my grandparents, aunts, uncles, and cousins. Even though we were financially poor, we were rich in spirit, and going to church was a big part of our lives. We prayed a lot, and she always told me that God had something special planned for my life. Today I remain very close with my mom and my stepfather, Valton Williams.

My mom raised me in this trailer in Warrenton, North Carolina. She drove a paneled Ford Pinto. We lived across the street from her parents, Esther and Alfred Coleman.

"He needs to go home and eat," Mom said.

"But he's hungry!" I told her. "He needs to eat."

She also remembers that, "If we had four hamburgers on the Hibachi Grill, I'd eat one, Cedric would eat one, and he'd give the rest to whomever else he had invited over to eat. Mind you, this happened at a time when I didn't have enough money for his lunch, which cost 50 cents."

When Mom got home from school, my friends would be in the house — even though we were supposed to play outside.

"Miss King is coming!" they exclaimed, scattering like ants to get outside.

"Miss King is coming!"

"Miss King is coming!"

"Miss King is coming!"

My mother would drive up and see all these guys in our yard.

"Early on," my mom recalls, "Cedric was like the Pied Piper with all these kids following him. They were his buddies. But when I was coming home from work, tired, I'd ask him, 'Why are all these children here, Cedric?'"

"Mom, you need to talk to such and such."

"They need to go home. They have a mother and father."

"No, their parents don't talk to them. Talk to them, Mom!"

Now she realizes the value of her presence to talk with my friends and give them guidance about life that they weren't getting at home. At the same time, my mom was aware of the neighborhood bullies.

"We had a cedar tree in our yard that looked like a Christmas tree," she says. "They told Cedric they were going to cut the tree down. Cedric had a kitten. They threatened to kill the kitten."

One of the bullies was on the basketball team.

"I'd go pick up Cedric," Mom says. "Sometimes he'd offer to give the bully a ride home. And I said, 'Cedric, we barely have enough gas to take us home.' And he's asking me to drive other people to their homes. So, I just said, 'Okay, Lord, that's Cedric's giving heart.'"

When the bullies found out that I lost my legs, they went to my mom with tears in their eyes and said, "Miss King, we've been praying for Cedric. How is he doing?"

My mom is a great example of the closest, best support you can have.

"Cedric, don't settle for anything less than what you want in life," she always told me. "You're wonderful. You're great. You're smart. You can do anything you want to do."

FATHER FIGURES

My dad was a good dude, but after my parents divorced when I was small, he had things he was trying to work out as I was growing up. Meanwhile, I was being guided by the powerful force of the women in my life: my mom, my aunts, and my grandmothers.

Several father figures taught me how to think and act like a gentleman. These influential men showered me with an abundance of love and guidance.

My mother's father, whom I call Papa, and her three brothers, Charles, Arnett, and Douglas, were super helpful. I visited their homes and was close to their kids, my cousins. Uncle Charles was almost like my surrogate dad. He took me bike riding and target shooting, and he gave me my first talk on manhood. He even gave me a book for boys called, *What's Happening to my Body?* by Lynda Madaras.

During my senior year of high school, I told my mother, "Ma, I know you can't afford to send me to college, and I want to go to college one day, so I'm going to join the Army."

Uncle Charles, a senior airman in the US Air Force with his wife, Oita, came to our house to sit with me when the Army recruiters visited. My grandfather was there, too, but Charles was the hands-on person.

"I was very blessed to have these supportive men in our family for Cedric," my mom says now. "They were like my husbands."

Her new husband — my former teacher and basketball coach — also became my stepfather. Here's how it happened: Mr. Valton Williams was my fifth-grade teacher at North Warren Elementary School. My mom's first memory of hearing about Mr. Williams happened when I came home from school and said:

"Mr. Williams said we have to get rid of all of our drugs."

"Excuse me, our what?" Mom asked.

"Ma, Tylenol and aspirin are drugs."

"Cedric, I don't know what this man is teaching you."

"Ma, they're considered over-the-counter drugs."

Now my mother remembers how she convinced me that over-the-counter drugs were okay to have in the house, regardless of what I'd learned in Mr. Williams' health and physical education classes.

"Mr. Williams was a strong force in Cedric's life since fifth grade," Mom says. "By sixth grade, I knew he was interested in me. But I said, there's no way I'm going to date my son's teacher. When Cedric transitioned to another school for seventh grade, I said, 'Okay, I can go out with you.'"

I graduated from high school in June on one weekend of 1995, and walked my mom down the aisle the next weekend.

"I didn't want to marry until Cedric graduated," Mom says. "I wanted to close that book with raising Cedric. Valton has a daughter, Tiara, so we jokingly say we have a son and a daughter."

The following month, in July of 1995, I went to the Army. When I came home to visit, I still called Valton "Coach" because he coached my basketball team.

My mother remembers how Valton would tell me to talk about certain things with my father, who was living in Warrenton. "But Cedric would sit with Valton longer than with his father. I'd walk in when they were watching a game on TV and just talking, and I'd say, 'Son, didn't you come by to spend time with me?' and he'd say, 'Yeah, Ma, but look at this play!' and they would proceed to referee and coach the entire game. I just felt blessed that Valton and my brothers have been such strong father figures for Cedric."

ANOTHER FATHER FIGURE: UNCLE GEORGE

Uncle George and I were always close, but once we learned about our mutual interest in books like *The Power of Your Subconscious Mind* by Joseph Murphy, *The Power of Positive Thinking* by Dr. Norman Vincent Peale, *The Compound Effect* by Darren Hardy, and *Think and Grow Rich* by Napoleon Hill, it was on!

"I'm thinking about becoming a motivational speaker after I retire from the Army," I told Uncle George. Fast forward to my time in Walter Reed, and Uncle George surmises, "He had already purposed that that was what he wanted to do before he got injured. Once he got his mind right — that I am still here, and I should do something with what God has gifted me with — I know that in talking with him, he went through a lot of soul-searching in the hospital. His identity was all tied in the military and what he could accomplish physically. Originally, he struggled with feelings of 'WHAT AM I NOW?' What could he do as an Army Ranger… until he came to grips with the fact that he had a very powerful testimony. He once said to my wife, Carolyn, 'How do I know that my legs weren't my handicap? God had to take my handicap away.'"

I learned how to completely transform my thinking to my advantage by absorbing the wisdom of strong male role models like Uncle George. When we're kids, we don't think about things like role models. But now I know that God chose the right family for me. He placed all these people around me to serve as teachers, so that I could grow into someone who teaches others how to develop mental and physical toughness, persevere past pain, and see blessings in the obstacles.

They also taught me how to act, so that one day I could convince an amazing woman like Khieda to become my wife. These lessons started when Uncle George and Aunt Carolyn modeled behavior for me as a kid. He demonstrated how to be a gentleman without sitting me down and giving me a book on etiquette. Uncle George made a conscious effort to show me, *This is how you treat a woman,* by his behavior toward Aunt Carolyn.

They did this during their courtship at times when they could have been out dancing, dining, going to the movies, or doing anything else. Instead, they chose to come visit me, a little kid, their nephew, on a date! They were aiming for something so much bigger than themselves, and they understood the power of providing love and support for someone who needed it, but did not know it, and could not ask for it.

Everything we do every day is modeling a message for others. What message are you sending by your behavior? Are you exuding confidence and courage? If not, who's someone you can emulate as how you'd like to be?

With Uncle George and Aunt Carolyn as a kid (left). As a tall teenager with Uncle George.

He or she may not even know that they're serving as a model for your better self. Sometimes we don't even know we're encouraging others to succeed. I had no idea that the two women in the medical tent at Mile 18 of my first Boston Marathon were inspired to not quit the race and instead keep going to the finish line — because they saw me walk out of the tent on my prosthetic legs and push myself to the end. I didn't know that the lady in church who heard me say I wanted to climb Stone Mountain would actually be there alongside us and witness the power of doing the daring thing that you say you're going to do.

We don't know what effect we're having on those around us unless they tell us. Strangers usually don't speak up. Nobody around me at the airport would know I was suffering from excruciating pain, because rather than grimacing and announcing to the world how much I'm hurting, I smile and pray, thanking God for my wife and daughters, to distract myself from the unrelenting pain.

This plugs me into the "give-get wavelength;" something good always happens after I smile through the pain. This is my way of modeling the behavior that feeds the continuous cycle of giving and receiving.

Be the support for others that you want for yourself. When I'm in pain and muster up the strength to smile at a stranger, and he or she smiles back or even speaks kind words that distract me from my suffering, then I am giving what I need and it comes back on me.

A simple smile is so powerful! For you, and for the person who receives it. We all need that human connection. Say hello to everyone you interact with. Ask their name. That little attention might just be the positive boost they need to get through the day.

You never know. That person may have made a bet with himself that if nothing good happens that day, then he will take his own life. Then boom, your smile and kind words could uplift him into a healthier mindset.

So plug into the "give-get wavelength" of support. It will help you and everyone around you.

More Love and Support from Aunt Karen and Uncle Mac

Aunt Karen, one of my mom's sisters, climbed Stone Mountain with us on my Alive Day.

"A couple of times," she recalls, "it was a little frightening because we're thinking, 'Is he gonna slip?' He climbed it. It's tough enough to climb Stone Mountain when you have two good legs. It was something he had to do. It was amazing, and it was wonderful when he got to the top."

Aunt Karen and Uncle Mac have two daughters, Karissa, who's three years younger than me, and Khristina, who's six years younger than me. I was like a big brother for my cousins as we were growing up. When Khristina was six, they took me on a family trip to Disney World.

"My legs are tired," she said as we walked around the giant park.

So I carried her around on my back. As I got older, and was far away from them, especially during deployments, I continued to support my cousins by giving them advice about life, men, and themselves. I wrote to them often, with messages like this:

A LETTER TO KARISSA
Pay attention to this Karissa

1. *Be aggressive with your love life.*

2. *Don't let today pass saying, "I will do it tomorrow."*

3. *Count your blessings when times are bad.*

4. *Be a role model to your friends.*

5. *Boys/men will respect you just as you are.*

6. *Don't wait until you are 35 to find love.*

7. *Accept that God might not give you a full house on your first hand.*

8. *Don't be listening to oldies all the time.*

9. *Learn one good pickup line and then master it. You never know when you'll need it.*

10. *Don't meet the guy of your dreams in a nightmarish place.*

11. *When tithing, recite Malachi 3:10 and have faith that it will come to pass.*

P.S. Guys say really smooth things, but the smoothest guys let your good intuition do the talking.

Here's a letter I sent from the Middle East:

A LETTER TO KARISSA AND KHRISTINA

I know you guys must have been told that I am home because I haven't gotten a package in a while. Please send:

1. *Burn 2 CDs with songs from R Kelly, Kirk Franklin, Aretha Franklin, Mary J Blige's new album, Cece Winans, Al Green, Mariah Carey, Busta Rhymes, Erykah Badu, Beyonce's new album, Donny Hathaway, and any more gospel and R&B you can think of. Please, please send. I need new music and not rap so much - just good old school or gospel.*

2. *Pictures from the family reunion.*

3. *Gardetto's, you know the chips I used to eat up during the summers from the Walmart around the corner on Wesley Chapel.*

4. *A letter telling me about the last couple of months.*

5. *Some tapes from church. Tell Uncle Mac and Aunt Karen the fellows like listening to them.*

6. *The Jet and Ebony magazines I missed since March. Tell Uncle Mac the sports section and the comic strips.*

7. *All your love and support.*

8. *Tell Uncle Mac and Aunt Karen that if they see any new or old men's books, please send them.*

9. *Call Khieda and check on her.*

I will be home soon. I love you and I want you to know that you mean a lot to me and we will always be tight — unless you don't send this package.

P.S. — See if you can track down the pre-cooked bacon.

SUPPORT IN THE FORM OF PROTECTION

I started feeling uneasy as I anticipated the first time my sister-cousin Jennifer visited me at Walter Reed. When she came in the room, I gave her a hug, we visited for a while, and then I just broke down and cried my eyes out.

"Why are you crying?" she asked.

"I don't want you to see me weak like this."

I was not yet okay with me. I was ashamed of how I looked. Ashamed because I needed help all the time. Ashamed because I had no legs. I wasn't physically Cedric like I was before. I thought my identity was tied up in what I lost. It was tough on me for my family members to see me, and this especially hit home when I saw Jennifer.

Turns out, for all my uneasiness and insecurity about how she would see me without legs, I later learned that she was having similar feelings.

"I remember when I walked in," she recalls, "all that fear, that nervousness just went away because I was looking at Cedric, and he was alive and very coherent. It was almost as if nothing had happened. Granted, he didn't have any legs. His right arm was bandaged up, but he was in very good spirits. He was ecstatic to see me, and from that moment on I thought, 'Okay, he lost his legs, but he's still Cedric,' and that made it a lot easier to accept what had happened. It was amazing. He looked the same. When he did break down, he started apologizing. 'I'm supposed to be the one to protect you. I'm your protector, and I can't protect you anymore.' I told him, 'You'll always be my brother; you'll always be there to protect me. You need to be crying that you're alive — that you're still here to protect me!'"

In our big family, we were both our single mothers' "only child." We lived in trailers next door to each other, and we were like brother and sister.

My cousin Jennifer Smith was my constant companion as a child; we are close in age and we still enjoy a brother-sister bond.

"We used to fight like cats and dogs," Jennifer remembers. "Then I'd go to my house, and he'd go to his house, and the next day we were best friends again."

Jennifer was a tomboy because she would do whatever I wanted to do. Sometimes we'd take spoons and dig holes in our yard and pretend we were filming a commercial with our Tonka trucks. Sometimes we'd hang upside down on the clothesline pole and just talk. We'd go through the Sears or the J.C. Penney catalog and pick out one thing from every page that we wanted, with zero expectation that our working-class moms could afford what we'd circled. We'd climb trees after a rainstorm, and one of us would shake the branches to make the water rain down.

"I don't remember there being a time when he wasn't around," Jennifer says. "We spent so much time together. That's the closest an only child can have to a sibling. We were very protective of each other."

Seeing Jennifer for the first time in the hospital forced me to question whether I could now protect her from the bullies in her grown-up life. *Could I protect my wife? My daughters?*

It was tough. Today, I wish I could go back and tell myself, "You're still intact, bro! You are better than you were because you've gone through this thing that's going to elevate your character and your personality. You may have been boisterous, outgoing, and comical before, but you're going to be even more so because of this!"

As family members came to see me, all my dread melted away as I saw again and again that they were okay with me and how I looked. The best thing? They were treating me like the old Cedric.

That was a powerful epiphany, because I realized that who I am has always been more valuable than what I lost. Who I am remained unchanged. Who you are will never die. What you have will get old, disappear, pass away. Who you are on the inside — your spirit, your personality, your uniqueness — is the part of you that makes people smile. That's what matters.

The legs weren't making people smile. The legs weren't inspiring people. When I realized that what people care about are my actions and my words, I started letting go of the fear and shame. I relaxed into my new reality with peace and acceptance. And I became determined to become the best version of the new me.

That would take determination, something Jennifer says I've had from an early age.

"When I got a 10-speed bike, I left my old, smaller bike outside," she recalls. "It rained on that old bike to the point that one of the handlebars rusted off. One day Cedric and I were outside, fiddling around, looking for something to do. We pull out that bike. I said to Cedric, 'Why don't you ride this bike and jump over this dirt pile?' Our street came around a corner and down a hill and there was a dirt pile at the bottom. I said, 'I bet you can't ride this bike and pop a wheelie over this dirt pile.' He, of course, had to prove to me that he could, so he took the bike up to the top of the hill and he rode down. When he got to the dirt pile, he did pop a wheelie — then he flew off the bike! The bike went one way, and his body the other. It knocked the wind out of him. I panicked and started screaming, 'I think he's dead!' He gets up, he kind of catches his breath, and we look at each other and just die laughing!'"

This story illustrates one powerful truth about me.

"If somebody tells him he can't," she says, "his attitude is, 'I'm going to show them that I can.' That attitude has been instrumental in who he is today. Cedric is always very determined and persistent. I think if people knew where he came from, they'd see he's just your average guy, this little boy who grew up with a single mom in a poor town in North Carolina without a lot of money and with nothing ever handed to him. Everything he has, he's worked for; people might think and understand, *Oh, he's kind of just like me.* He had dreams, and he didn't let anyone tell him no. Cedric is a classic case of 'If you hear 10 no's, on the eleventh try, you may get a yes.' If you just look at his background, you see he's very relatable. He grew up watching cartoons after school, just like everybody else. He grew up wishing his mom could buy him all the new clothes and the latest gadgets. Reality didn't allow him to hold himself back. Those circumstances didn't dictate where he went with his life, and that having legs or no legs doesn't dictate who you are or where you can go."

Your Support Will Rise to the Occasion

Kelly Alston and Kenya Solomon came into my life in high school. Both were originally from New York — Brooklyn and Queens, respectively — which gave them instant credibility in our small, Southern town.

Kelly and I played on the basketball team together, and from tenth grade on, we were like brothers. If you saw one of us, you saw the other. If Kelly dated a girl, I dated her best friend or her sister. We were like a package deal. Kenya joined us in twelfth grade, and the three of us became inseparable. I was also very close with both Kelly's and Kenya's families. Kelly and Kenya were the brothers I never had.

Kelly tried to talk me into going to college, but I had made up my mind to join the Army. He and Jennifer went to the same college, so when I was at Fort Bragg, I always went up to Greensboro and hung out on the weekends with their college friends, sleeping in Kelly's dorm room. Sunday nights, I returned to the base. This went on for two years.

After the Army sent me to Tacoma, Washington, when Kelly got married, I flew to his wedding after getting someone to cover my post. I learned the hard way that that was not the way to go about it. I was considered AWOL, lost a rank, and got in big trouble.

Looking back, my dedication to my friendship with Kelly was so important to me. It exemplifies the healthy balance of giving and receiving support. Years earlier in high school, Kelly finished classes at lunch time, but I skipped an English class every day to hang out with him.

One day he dropped me off at home. My mom was there, and she was furious. The school had called her to report that I was failing English. Both she and Kelly started yelling at me. Kelly demanded, "Are you skipping English?" I had been making poor decisions based on my mindset that my friends were more important than my schoolwork.

As a result, when my friends went to college, I decided school was not for me, and I joined the Army. Kenya didn't know anyone who had served in the military, so he was anxious about whether the experience might change me.

"Cedric saw crazy stuff," he says now, "but he never wore it."

I never let it show because that has never been my personality. I've always been too focused on making other people feel good.

"Cedric makes everyone feel like they're the most important person in the world," Kenya adds, "even when he's tired or when there are people waiting. He's right there with you. I've never seen anyone do it like he does it."

About 10 years ago, Kenya inspired me to start reading personal development books and listening to CD's. Everything I learned works in tandem with my faith to get me through tough moments. This laid a deeper foundation for cultivating mental toughness and believing that every adversity is a set-up for success.

"When Cedric left on that final deployment," Kenya recalls, "we were both in a very positive frame of mind of whatever it takes, keep low; it's all good. We always kept a positive vibe amongst the reality of 'Hey, this is gonna be tough.' Gloom and doom never entered our minds because we had this mindset of faith, abundance, and perseverance. Never was it, 'Oh man, what am I going to do?'"

THE BEST LOVE & SUPPORT: TREAT ME LIKE CEDRIC

Both Kelly and Kenya's handling of me in Walter Reed when they first saw me was a testament to how well they knew me, and I wish everyone could follow their example. Kelly drove up from Charlotte to see me, and when he walked in the room, I was sleeping.

"You can go ahead and wake him," Khieda said. "He's been waiting to see you all day."

Kelly slapped me on the head and said, "Wake up! Wake up!"

I looked at Kelly; Kelly looked at me. I smiled, grabbed him, hugged him, and we cried for probably five minutes. We were just hugging each other. We spoke no words. We just looked at each other.

"You know I'm going to be all right?" I said.

"I have no doubt," Kelly said. "Cedric, you're not going to let this beat you."

Today, Kelly says I gave him an overview of the whole accident. "It was like he was trying to convince me that he was going to be okay, but he was also trying to convince himself," Kelly recalls. "We talked, laughed, but mostly talked about old times. Yeah, he had been through this horrific accident, but he didn't want pity or anyone feeling sorry for him. It happened. It is what it is, and he was going to be okay."

Kelly treated me like the guy in high school who used to mix it up during a basketball game by wearing two different shoes and socks pulled up over his calves, when nobody else was doing that. He treated me like the Cedric who was always laughing and joking. He treated me as the king of snacks, as the first person he ever saw make his own dip. He considered me a dip expert, and I'm the guy who got him hooked on sour cream mixed with French onion soup mix.

That guy lying in the bed at Walter Reed was the same guy he knew, and Kelly didn't hesitate or consider treating me like anything but who I was.

Neither did Kenya.

When he got the call from Khieda that my legs had been amputated, his first thought was "of this guy I used to play ball with on the dirt court — the guy always gave it his all. I thought, 'Okay, we can work it out.' I broke down after I got off the phone, asking, 'What does this mean for my friend? What is my friend now going to face?' I had seen my own father come back from impossible odds, so I tried to reassure myself... *but this is my guy!*"

Kenya remembers: "I drive up to Walter Reed, and before I go into the room, his mom and Khieda tell me they're leaving and to make sure his pillow's fluffed, that he has a glass of water, and to take care of him. I say, 'Okay.' Then I walk in the room and he has this piece-of-cheese-shaped foam thing elevating his arm, and he looks skinny, and my first thought is: *I'm not doing any of that! I'm not going to treat him any differently than the guy I've known forever. I'm not going to treat him any differently!* I said, 'Yo, man, what are you doing? Get up! Why are you lying down? It's DC, we need to get out!'"

I sent Kenya out to get some white chocolate Kit Kats and Reese's Peanut Butter Cups.

"I'm driving around on a mission to get him his candy," Kenya recalls. "I get back to his room, and we're sitting there playing music. We start playing *A Tribe Called Quest*, rapping all the lyrics at the top of our voices like it didn't matter! We still knew the lyrics. We had a sense of *Yo, we still got this! We still know something good.* We just had this amazing time. We had the best time. It was a celebration."

Here were two of my closest friends coming to see me in the hospital. The best thing they did was treat me like the Cedric they knew and loved. I don't consider it a coincidence that both Kelly and Kenya acted that way when they saw me. They provided the ultimate support for my mental and physical healing, because they convinced me that I was the same old Cedric. If they had treated me differently, it would have reinforced the struggle I was having. Instead, they convinced me that I was still fun, still lovable, still their friend. And that helped me regain my confidence and heal.

My wife and daughters mean the world to me. Photo credit: Kent Horner.

How To Celebrate Life And Love

CREATE YOUR PERSONALIZED CELEBRATION. My family created a special day to celebrate my survival. They organized my Alive Day with a cookout, music, and lots of fun. Think about how you can create a personalized event to commemorate your success in overcoming a tough challenge. Make it something really meaningful. Describe it here:

_____

_____

_____

_____

ARE YOU RESISTING SUPPORT? Are you ready and willing to accept the support that you need? Why might you be resisting it? What can you do to accept help?

_____

_____

_____

_____

RELEASING SHAME AND FEAR. Do you feel ashamed of your situation? Are you worried that people will treat you differently? Explore your feelings, and look for evidence from your friends, family, and colleagues that shows that they love you no matter what your challenge might be.

_____

_____

_____

_____

WHAT YOU GIVE, YOU RECEIVE. Think about how you've been supportive and loving for others in your past. This will show you that you've been sowing seeds for others, and now in your time of need, that will all come back to you in the form of love and assistance from others.

_____

_____

_____

_____

PROCEEDING WITH CONFIDENCE. If you are lacking confidence to turn your breaking point into your Making Point, who can you enlist to help you brainstorm ways to boost your confidence? Write down the exact words you'll use to ask that person to help you.

_____

_____

_____

_____

WHO ARE YOU, REALLY? I was afraid that my injury would change the way my friends and family perceived me and treated me. But they loved me for me, not for my legs. It forced me to think about who I am, really. So, who are you? Not your job, your education, your possessions, or your awards. Who are you as a person?

_____

_____

_____

_____

7

Trusting Your Team

Enlisting to Join a Never-Ending Team

God has been preparing me to face my Making Point all my life. Even before I was born, God had a huge plan for my life. I trust that now more than ever. But as a kid and teenager, I was just working with what I had — and *didn't* have — to make a decision about the next step in my future.

God is the ultimate Commander-in-Chief of my life, and he was dictating my marching orders in the fall of 1994 when, at the beginning of twelfth grade, I decided to join the Army. College was not an option; my SAT scores were dismal, and my grades were hardly impressive. That was the price I was paying for giving all my attention to girls, basketball, and fun throughout high school. Since I was not a strong student, I did not want to waste my mother's money on tuition at a community college. I wanted to earn my own way, and when I was ready, get my own apartment, and make something of myself.

I saw joining the Army as a way of helping me do that. My decision was totally off the script and not influenced by anyone. Growing up in a poor part of North Carolina, if you're in an underserved community, military recruiters seek you out. They know that if you're not going to college, then statistically, you're probably going to jail, or you're going to hang around until your life spirals downward.

I wanted to rise up and out of the poverty and struggles that I saw in the small town around me. No wars were going on; it seemed like a safe time to serve four years in the military. So, in July of 1995, at the age of 17, I enlisted, and headed off to Basic Training in Fort Jackson, South Carolina, three hours from where I grew up.

Back then, I had no idea that 20-plus years later, I would be standing on prosthetic legs on stages across America and the world, sharing my story to help people blast past obstacles and become their best.

Enlisting in the military was a crucial step toward getting here. Joining the Army put me on a team that made me bigger, better, and stronger.

That's why I want to talk with you about joining a team, and trusting your team to help you become the best version of yourself.

Discovering A New Definition of Success

I had no vision, and no plan, beyond joining the military. I sure didn't expect for the Army to become a catalyst for Cedric King to discover his true potential. The whole process became like a giant mirror that made me look at myself in a new way. It made me take a closer look at my thinking, my physical strength, my intelligence, my value, and my reputation amongst my peers and our military leaders.

I arrived fresh out of high school, where the playing field had not been level: everybody knew the smart kids, the popular kids, the low achievers, and so on. I recognized immediately that in the Army, we were all equal. This was eye-opening!

The mindset I carried from high school was that the golden boys and golden girls were predestined for the spotlight, achievement, and praise. For instance, everybody knew who the prom king and queen would be before they were chosen. Those regaled positions came from a certain pool of people. I was not in that pool.

When graduation approached, no lottery or election determined who would be the valedictorian: everybody knew. In high school, a pool of smart people earned the good grades, the honors, the praise from teachers, the college scholarships. I was not in that pool, either. This led me to equate success with being in the National Honor Society. That was totally out of reach for me; therefore, I was not successful. Or so I had conditioned myself to believe, and accepted that as my reality.

The Army smashed that belief, thank God! There, success was not measured by my GPA; it was determined by many other factors. And everyone had the same opportunity to achieve these. The military is all about protocols and following a strict chain of command, from Private up to the President, the Commander-in-Chief.

In the Army, nobody played favorites. I loved that. The other soldiers were my peers, my equals, and we stood shoulder-to-shoulder and toe-to-toe as a unit. Accepting that I was no different — no better, no worse — enabled me to begin releasing some very limiting beliefs about myself and about others.

In basic training, I learned fast that either you're going to try hard or it's going to be very trying for you. If you don't give it your all, you will suffer. That made my path easy because I don't like suffering. My only option was to try harder. And without the constraints of, *Well, I'm not a 4.0*, or *I'm not prom king*, the world was my oyster and I could start fresh.

As a result, I stood out at the very beginning during our Basic Training Physical Fitness Test, which we called PT. To graduate from boot camp and move up to Advanced Infantry Training, every soldier must pass these physical tests that evaluate their fitness level. PT has three components: at least 35 push-ups in two minutes; no less than 47 sit-ups in two minutes; and a two-mile run with a maximum time of 16 minutes and 36 seconds. We had to score at least 150 points, with a minimum of 50 points in each category. The maximum score was 300 points.

PT was all about physical endurance, which is fueled by mental strength. I learned that during my high school basketball days. When I toughened my mind to block out the noise of the crowd, as well as my own performance anxiety and whatever else was trying to cloud my brain, I played my best games.

Now in the Army, I crushed PT. God blessed me with natural physical strength, and people noticed right away. Verbal accolades and pats on the back came first.

Here's the catch: I was not familiar with the feeling of standing out amongst 100 of my peers as a 17-year-old. Outside of my family, no one had ever told me I was significant. Suddenly, new emotions and possibilities surged through me.

Man, I'm good at this…?

You mean I stand out from the crowd of strangers?

Man, this feels good! Let me try harder!

I loved the praise, and I wanted more! It was addictive. So, I tried harder, improved exponentially, and launched into an upward momentum that felt like success.

This is the new start I need!

This was significant in the scheme of things: I decided for myself to join the Army, and now I was being rewarded for that decision. I liked it!

Again, this was all new to me: I had never been singled out for being exceptional. Making varsity basketball two years in a row was a pretty big deal in high school. I was required to maintain a certain GPA to stay on the team. I exerted the minimum effort to do that, and I certainly wasn't aiming for the highest GPA. I did *just enough* to stay on the team.

And now the military comes along and says, *There's something special about you, young man,* and that felt fantastic. I wanted to feel more and more fantastic, so I ran faster, did more push-ups, and did more sit-ups.

I vividly remember the first time I was singled out for being exceptional: I was named *Soldier of the Month.*

Then one day, in the middle of a formation, a Colonel approached me and said:

"Private King, you know I'm going to beat you today on this run."

I sort of laughed, and said respectfully, "We're gonna see, sir."

Do you know what happened? I outran him!

Afterwards, my Sergeant came up to me, and said, "The Colonel wants to see you." The equivalent of this in a business setting would be the CEO asking to talk with the intern.

"King," the Colonel said when I went to see him. "Come in. Close the door."

I followed his instructions.

"Young man," he said, "you've got a lot of potential."

I sat there looking at him in awe, thinking, *All I did was run fast.*

Again, I had to shift my mindset. If I played a good game of basketball in high school, my English teacher was not going to compliment me. In the military, the physical-mental connection is unified. They believe that if you can push yourself physically, it's effort. Physical effort powered by mental effort. Physical strength and mental strength are one in the same.

This positive recognition sparked a ravenous hunger inside me to become the best Cedric King possible. I worked hard to run at maximum speed, and to push through pain and fatigue to do as many push-ups and sit-ups as my body would allow. Basic training required us to work out hard, five days a week. This established a regimen that I continued during deployments. Our goal was to be physically and mentally strong. It's so easy to give up when your lungs are aching, your muscles are burning, and you're tired. That's when you have to tap into your mental strength. Your brain is like a powerful battery for your body. Of course, you have to eat high-quality foods for fuel, stay hydrated, and get enough sleep. But when you exhaust those fuel sources, it's time to plug into your brain power.

If you believe you can do one more push-up, or run another mile, then your body will respond accordingly. When you exert yourself more every day, you reach a tipping point where your mental prowess and your muscles get into a continuous cycle of pushing each other. Before you know it, you'll be setting your own personal records.

My military career was a chain of *Let me see what else I can do — not to show off, but to set myself apart from the person I was in high school. Let me tack on something that I didn't think I could be good at.* That felt fantastic, and motivated me like rocket fuel.

GETTING STUCK AT A DESK JOB

When you're pumped with rocket fuel, and ready to catapult into the adventure of physical and mental challenges, getting stuck at a desk job is a recipe for misery. That's what happened to me. And it all goes back to when I signed up for the Army with that recruiter back in high school.

"According to your test scores," he had told me, "here are the jobs you can take..."

Meanwhile, my family was advising me to: "Pick a job where you can sit behind a desk. Use your mind, not your back."

So, when I finished Basic Training, and it was time to embark on the remainder of my four years of service, I was placed in a job working with the aviation department, helping pilots log flight hours. As an Aviation Operations Specialist, I had a nice, easy desk job. I could relax, kick back, and take it easy.

But sometimes you don't know something until you experience it.

I hated sitting behind a desk! I longed to return to the rigorous challenges of boot camp, and more. My heart was saying, *This is not what I want to do! I want to do the cool stuff! The tough stuff! I want to be an elite member of the infantry!*

Here again, I believe God instilled this drive inside me, to crave the challenge and adventure of becoming an infantry soldier. I wanted to put myself in rugged terrains like mountains, swamps, and woods. I craved the adrenaline rush of jumping out of airplanes, mastering obstacle courses, mastering sharpshooting, and battling bad guys, even if that meant traveling to combat zones. As my spirit soared with excitement, I realized that you don't pick your path; your path picks you. And for me, divine Providence was leading me.

In 1996, I was selected as a color guard rifleman, which meant I had to salute with my rifle, as part of the 18th Airborne Corps Change of Command for outgoing General Hugh Shelton and incoming Corps Commander General Jack Keane at a ceremony at Fort Bragg, NC.

On my first day in the Army, I didn't know my fullest potential. When I started scoring 300s on my PT, my excitement manifested in everything — giving more care and attention to my appearance and my uniform, learning more military history, and following protocols to a T.

Then as I sat behind that desk, I wondered, *What else could I do if I tried a little harder? What else am I capable of?* I didn't know, and I could never solve the mystery of this new calling until I broke free from the desk job.

I Wanted to Be at the Top

When I told my family that I wanted to leave the safety and comfort of my desk job and go tackle rugged terrains and handle weapons, my mom responded, "Who is this person? This is not the person that I raised."

"Ma, my true desire in the Army is to fight bad guys," I told her. "I can't work at a desk for the rest of my life. It's not for me."

She shook her head and said, "I love you. I just don't understand where this is coming from."

But I wasn't quite sure how to transition from where I was to where I wanted to be; the constant hum of *What's next?* ran through my mind. That's when God showed me my next step — in the chow hall. I met a guy there, and he wore a RANGER tab on his uniform.

"What's that on your shoulder?" I asked.

"My Ranger tab," he said. "I just finished Ranger School." He explained that he just spent 61 days in swamps, mountains, and forests, learning small-unit infantry combat tactics. "You've got to pass PT test, patrol, navigate, and then you graduate and get your Ranger tabs."

It sounded difficult, and that was music to my ears! Anybody who could survive all that had to be exceptional. All I could think was, *Sign me up!* I fell in love with the idea of becoming a Ranger. I had no clue what it required, but I was certain that it would provide the mental and physical challenges I craved, and lay the foundation for a solid Army career as I sported my own set of hard-earned Ranger tabs.

But, as with all things, I couldn't just jump from one to ten and be in Ranger School.

First, I had to change my Army status to "combat occupational specialty." My spirit soared at the idea of striving for something beyond what my test score in the Recruiter's office said I could, should, or would be good at doing. So, I followed my heart and changed to front-line foot soldier. I had no guarantee that I would ever get to Ranger School, let alone graduate, but I had to take that step and believe in a successful outcome.

Back in Sunday school, I had learned to walk by faith, not by sight, because Hebrews 11:1 says, "Now faith is the substance of things hoped for, the evidence of things not seen." When you have faith, God gives you the vision to see your maximum potential, and you have to hold that vision in your mind's eye as if it has already happened. And when you give praise, expressing gratitude as if you've already brought your vision into 3D reality, it's only a matter of time before you're actually experiencing it in real life.

Of course, there's a risk of failure. But I believe what Robert F. Kennedy once said: "Only those who dare to fail greatly can ever achieve greatly." It's better to try and fail than to never try at all. The old Cedric liked to take the path of least resistance. This new Cedric who was coming to life during my so-far short stint in the Army, wanted to embark on one of the toughest challenges in life. Army Rangers are the toughest of the tough. To get that way, they have to survive training that's grueling beyond description.

Here's a hint of just how tough it was: I declared that I wanted to become a Ranger in 1998. But it took six years to finally earn my Ranger tabs in 2004. During that time, every failure taught me something, and prepared me for success. And I learned to think like genius inventor Thomas Edison, who once said, "I have not failed. I've just found 10,000 ways that won't work."

Don't Fall in Love with the Finish Line

I became a Ranger on my third attempt. The struggle to earn my tabs taught me what holds most of us back from achieving our dreams: focusing on the finish line, and not paying attention to the journey. If the finish line is a diploma; well, you can't get your diploma without taking the classes. You can't pass the classes without doing the assignments. You can't do the assignments without dedicating time and attention to them. You can't be in the school without applying yourself!

If you focus too hard on your destination, you won't pay attention to every little step that's required to get there. You'll stumble. You'll crash. You'll miss signs and lessons along the way. And you'll fail. So, you have to begin at the starting line, and make peace with being there. That means, if you're embarking on a new workout regimen, and you can only do four push-ups on your first day, just accept that as your starting point. A master chef did not walk into the kitchen and create a gourmet meal when he or she first discovered a passion for cooking. It took years of schooling and practice to learn how to use the perfect herbs, the best temperature, and the greatest ingredients to create a culinary masterpiece.

That chef probably prepared some dishes early on that were downright disgusting. At that point, it's so easy to give up. Because as soon as we get a few steps down the road, the journey to our finish line is harder than we thought. So, we have to fall in love with step one before we can advance to step two, three, or ten. The path from one to ten is proof that the place exists; and that proof also confirms you can have what your heart desires.

I started at one in Ranger School. We were starved, sleep deprived, and put in combat simulations with gunfire and enemy attacks. We had to traverse icy lakes, scale mountains, and survive in the woods. It was rough! So rough, that I failed the first time. I was so focused on the finish line, I was not meticulous about executing every detail of every assignment and drill with the precision required to pass. After that, I was deployed to Iraq. I attended another school. I went to Ranger School a second time and broke my foot; I had to leave. I wanted to give up.

At one point in Ranger School, I was the class leader, so I was the last to sleep, and first to rise; I always knew the location of every soldier, and I could tick down every stat pertaining to our mission. One night, we had simulated combat training. During this exercise, after walking up a mountain for 20 hours in frigid weather, I stop with my 50 soldiers around 2:00 a.m. in a place where we're going to stop for the night. Some soldiers set up a small perimeter that's about a 12- or 15-foot triangle. We can't use fire, even though the temperatures are in the low 20s and our canteens are frozen. We're all freezing cold and dead tired. But we have to stay awake all night, and it's my responsibility to get everyone prepared for the simulated attack. Some of our guys are so exhausted, they fall down on their faces and go to sleep.

"Stand up!" I shout. "Stand up! You have to stay awake!"

A short time before dawn, I think everyone's awake as I'm taking log notes in the middle of the triangle. Little do I know, that as I'm draped with a poncho to minimize the light from my flashlight, which has a red lens, my second-in-command is asleep.

Rat-tat-tat! Gunfire pierces the silent darkness. The simulated attack has begun. Our instructors are somewhere in the distance, watching us through night vision goggles, so they can assess our activities — and my leadership skills.

All my soldiers are awake now. But about five simulated enemy guys overtake our perimeter from three directions. They take some of my guys prisoner.

The scene is chaos! It's almost sunrise, and the whole exercise is a failure.

Afterwards, an instructor pulls me aside. I learned an important lesson from that simulation: Sometimes when you're trying to do the right thing, you cannot allow men's lives to be in danger by your delegation. As a leader, sometimes you're the only one who cares the most.

Failure is not an option. But the bottom line was, I failed. Just like I had failed so many other things in my life. Thankfully, it was only a simulated attack, and my failure did not cost anyone's life. The gravity of this situation was a powerful learning experience. So many of us want to live without failing. You'll succeed so much more if you have that loss on your record.

"There is no better than adversity," Malcolm X once said. "Every defeat, every heartbreak, every loss, contains its own seed, its own lesson on how to improve your performance the next time."

That belief inspired me to return to Ranger School for a third time. I passed!

SIGNING UP FOR ANOTHER SIX YEARS

There is no "I" in Army. There is no "I" in team. Teamwork is everything in the Army, and in life. We have our teams at work. We have our teams of family. We have our social teams. We don't thrive in isolation, distrust, or fear. My success and confidence in the Army came from developing myself while trusting my team.

This was exhilarating; I couldn't get enough of it. So, I signed up for another six years because I was having so much fun learning. I liked the rules. I liked the structure. I liked the whole military life-style of working hard and being rewarded for it.

My first introduction to leadership in the Army came from trusting my team. Before that, the only time I'd been a leader had been in Sunday school.

During my enlistment at Fort Bragg, I was put in charge. My pre-conceived notion that a leader had to be mean melted away, as did my belief that leaders could not have friends.

When it was my turn to lead a march from point A to point B, I had been watching others lead me, so I figured, "Well, this isn't so bad; I could probably do this, too." I just did what everybody else did.

I marched as a leader with confidence. Often people think if you can march well, then you can lead: you can stand in front of people with confidence. I discovered that I could march and lead a lot of people and maintain my sense of identity and confidence.

I was in charge for two to three weeks, just long enough for us to have an inspection and do a good job. By the time I graduated and had my orders for my next assignment, I realized that had been the first time anybody had put me in charge of other soldiers. I was responsible for making sure everybody's uniform looked right; that they showed up on time; that they understood what the day's duties were going to be, among other things, like ensuring the bathrooms were clean.

The next time I was in front of soldiers, I had a chance to call cadence. To do this, you've got to have the physical ability to run and keep pace with 100 soldiers on step next to you. You must know enough cadences for a three- to five-mile run. You must sing loudly enough for everyone to hear you. All this while out of breath because you're running!

In May of 2011, before deploying to Afghanistan, I called cadence during the All American Division Run at Fort Bragg, North Carolina for 22,000 paratroopers of the 82nd Airborne Division. That requires yelling motivational soldier songs at the top of my lungs while running at an eight-minute-mile pace for miles. In May of 2014, I returned to the same role on my running blades. Coincidentally, these photos were taken in roughly the same exact spot.

All of this takes confidence, and it's an indicator of a leadership trait.

Calling cadence required overcoming my inner critic, and in that moment, the first time I did it, that meant being okay with who I was. I had experienced some successes, and I had to use those past successes as validation that I could take on this challenge and succeed.

This goes back to the theme of using small wins, small successes, to push yourself to take on bigger challenges, and trust that past success to propel you forward.

These leadership roles opened my eyes to something I was capable of, something I was good at, and something I wanted to do more. My leaders taught me how to be a good leader and a good follower. I knew how to take an order and I knew how to give an order. You cannot be a successful leader without understanding the dynamics of being a leader and taking instructions. Part of being on a team is being subservient.

If the leader can't take orders, the fabric of the team is destroyed. They think, *You're not like us.*

Again, this applies beyond the Army. In life and in business, you must lead by example. Then the team is more willing to do the job.

Loyalty is an Army value, along with duty, selfless service, honor, respect, and personal courage. If you want to be a great leader, you must embody those values.

TRUSTING YOUR TEAM WITH A 360° PERSPECTIVE

A funny thing happens when you have a trusting, cooperative relationship with your team: opportunities come to you. Throughout my Army career, as I've said, I had ideas about what direction I wanted to go, but Providence was always orchestrating my steps.

In life, in love, in business, and in the military, the Law of Attraction is at play. People come into our lives every day. Some pass through, some become part of our team, and some become part of our story. Colonel Cedric Carrington personifies this. I met him in early 2011, when I was in a leadership position. He's an example of the fact that our reputations precede us.

"I'd heard of him and his enthusiasm for everything," says Colonel Cedric Carrington, who was a Battalion Commander at the time. "I needed him to help perpetuate this positive culture and image across the battalion. Lots of the soldiers in the battalion were tired, exhausted after several tough deployments. I was interested in getting some good leaders who understood my vision who could implement the vision at a lower level. I was looking for people with values and who could put the sense of worth and belonging back into the unit."

When Colonel Carrington asked me to join him, I agreed.

"We needed the right person with the right attitude," Colonel Carrington says. "I knew he would like a challenge. He took it head on. He was an accountable, engaged leader. He was out running and leading the run. He led from the front by example. I could see the team forming within a month. The organization I was most worried about became the organization I was least worried about. He rose to the occasion, and it became an effective, efficient platoon. Cedric is more action than words. He didn't let any member of his platoon beat him at anything. He was inspiring and motivating. He's what we look for in all leaders in the Army."

THAT DESK JOB

When I started that desk job, I had tasted what the Army had to offer me. I had found my place, but I had yet to find that thing that would sustain the singing in my heart that came from standing out.

I quickly learned that I didn't want to be a regular guy.

I believe everybody has something in them that will never be quiet when it comes to being exceptional. Not one of us wants to be just part of the crew. Everybody wants to be extraordinary. But we're hypnotized to accept *not* going after something that feels right when we're ensconced in the safety of what feels comfortable, the safety in that numeric formation, amidst an army of people who are regular. That provides no safety. That provides no life.

When we start listening to that voice inside that says, "You are created for much more than this," we begin to see opportunities. Our paths lead us in different directions when we start listening.

I discovered that sitting at that desk was my own sense of mediocrity; it was my path of least resistance. I had bought into a lie that I'd sold myself. I heard voices of frustration and doubt, but I'd had a peek into a level playing field from which I could spring forward fast. The path of least resistance will lead you off course. However, attacking the obstacle will inspire growth in you that will support you so much more than you can imagine in the low moments.

We all love being on top, enjoying a beautiful view and laughter and income and blessings and grace. When you are in the low times, you have to be most thankful because more things are growing down there. If you are mired in mediocrity, tell yourself you need some happier headlines. Tell yourself it's time to recalibrate.

Know this: you don't have to go anywhere outside of yourself to move forward. Everything you need is on the inside, just as it was for me. You have everything right now to become exceptional. You don't have to go find the magic potion. It's right there inside you.

Two quick ways to be exceptional: number one, do what you say you're going to do. Second: sit down and spend some time with yourself. We don't give ourselves time anymore. If you think you don't have time, make time. Then shut out the noise. It's easy to ignore your intuition when we are bombarded from the outside. So, turn off your phone, your computer, the music, and the TV. Get still and silent for a little while. Let your inner voice speak to you, and listen to its guidance. Your inner voice is your spirit, and it never steers you wrong.

It speaks the truth, because it knows what's best for you. It will warn you with a "gut feeling."

We don't have time enough **not** to do it.

You can call this meditation, prayer, or just being quiet. At first, your mind will jump around. So start at one minute. Start where you are.

This is so powerful. That lends itself to being all you can be; it's the truth. We can always start at one. Listen to the voice inside. The inside is the guru. It's your heart, helping you to tap into your power to become whatever you want to be.

RECRUITING YOUR WINNING TEAM

You're setting a major goal to accomplish something: heal from an injury, create a new life after divorce, earn your college degree, open a business, rebuild your life after bankruptcy, or recover from addiction. You can't do it alone. You need a team. Not just any team, but people who genuinely want to help you. So, let's recruit a winning team so you can accomplish your goal.

YOUR GOAL. Describe it, and why you need a team, in detail on the lines below.

_____

_____

_____

_____

YOUR CURRENT TEAM. Identify your core team of family, friends, colleagues, and community members. Consider a time when you have been 100 percent reliant on them or someone else. What did you tell yourself to trust them?

_____

_____

_____

_____

ACCEPTING HELP. Are you ready to accept help from a team? If not, why? Where might you resist help? Think of ways to push through that resistance.

_____

_____

_____

_____

TRUSTING STRANGERS. How can you interact with strangers to build a team of supporters? Write ways that strangers have helped you in the past. How have you ever helped a stranger? How did you feel? How can the experience of helping someone else, enable you to trust that a stranger would genuinely want to help you?

_____

_____

_____

_____

EXPERTS. What aspects of achieving the goal require help from others? What expertise do you need on your team? For example, you may need a lawyer to help you with your divorce, a credit counselor after bankruptcy, or a support group for your addiction. Make a list of key players that you need on your team.

_____

_____

_____

_____

RESOURCES. What organizations, grants, classes, products, or services could help you? Who can you recruit to your team to help you find and acquire these resources?

_____

_____

_____

_____

A MANTRA. Write something that you can repeat to encourage yourself that you will connect with the best team, such as, "The people I need are looking for me," or "Thank you God for the perfect people and resources to help me achieve my goals."

_____

_____

_____

_____

HOW YOU CAN HELP YOUR TEAM. Teams should be built on win-win relationships. So, describe how you can help the people on your team. Ask yourself, "What's in it for them?"

_____

_____

_____

_____

TIMEFRAME. Is your team offering lifetime membership? Or do you need a specific team to achieve a short term goal? Describe the lifespan of your team, and what needs to happen before it can disband.

_____

_____

_____

_____

ACTION. What are the roles and responsibilities of each team member? Write a summary of what you and each person will do.

_____

_____

_____

_____

PAST ACHIEVEMENTS. Make a list of challenges that you've overcome in the past. These enabled you to build a legacy of courage and perseverance that you can draw upon as you embark on your new goals. Who was on your team then? What did they teach you about teamwork?

_____

_____

_____

_____

SUCCESS! Describe the victorious result of what your team will achieve together. Whether it's earning a degree and attending graduation, or marking the one-year anniversary of your new business, or throwing an Alive Day party after a traumatic injury, write how you will feel and how you will celebrate.

_____

_____

_____

_____

8

Knowing Your Strength

PUSH YOURSELF OUT OF YOUR COMFORT ZONE

Your comfort zone might sound like a nice place. You feel safe, relaxed, and cozy there. But your comfort zone is not a place where you want to stay. It's not helping you. It's actually hurting you. It's holding you back.

In some ways, the hospital was a comfort zone for me. All my needs were met. They even brought me pancakes with extra syrup and melted butter the way I like it. I could have stayed in bed, watching TV, receiving visitors, and not even trying to walk or think about running. But I wanted to get as far away from an environment where everything was easy — and into a place where I would be forced to face problems that would show me just how tough the new version of myself could become.

Your mother's womb was a comfort zone. But to become an independent human being, you had to get pushed out into the world. You had to breathe, see, move, eat, walk, and think on your own. To become a fully functioning person, you have to leave the place where all your needs are automatically met and where you are completely safe.

I have always been a person who tries to escape my comfort zone. That's why I became an Army Ranger, and sought the toughest situations. Losing my legs was God's way of pushing me way, way out of any comfort zone I thought I had. With myself, with the Army, with my family and friends, and with the world. I embraced it, and it embraced me back, a million times over. Refusing to flee the oppression of your comfort zone — where you will not grow, learn, prosper, or become your best you who is fulfilling your God-given mission in life — is a crime you commit against yourself. You are robbing yourself of greatness. Health. Wealth. Love. Joy.

This year alone, I have pushed myself into some extreme *discom*fort zones, and I get stronger every time. I love it. I celebrate the pain, the perseverance, the difficulty. Because I know, like a chisel on a piece of marble, God is using that discomfort to hone me into the best Master Sergeant Cedric King that ever could walk this earth. The more I learn, the more I can teach. The better I become, the better I can help others become.

Wheelchair marathons and Ironman competitions are some of the extreme ways that I am shoving myself out of my comfort zone. I hope that this chapter inspires you to take bold action to abandon your comfort zone. If you don't, LIFE is going to do it for you. Whether you want to or not.

That means, if you don't get off the couch to exercise, you will probably gain weight and develop health problems like diabetes and hypertension that will cut your life short. Your comfort zone will make you sick and die early. How's that for motivation to escape your comfort zone!

Likewise, if you don't escape the so-called comfort zone of a dead relationship because you're afraid to leave and seek a better partner, then your heart will ache with sadness and you will rob yourself of the ultimate joy in life: true love.

If you never leave the day job that barely pays your bills because you're afraid, and as a result you never open the business that you dream about, you are robbing yourself of the infinite fortunes that you can earn as an entrepreneur.

We need to do things outside of our comfort zones, because they help us become a better version of who we are. The question is: are you willing to do the work? Here are some examples of how I'm doing the work, to inspire you to do the same, and reap the benefits that will transform your life into something exciting, amazing, and impactful.

AIRBORNE SCHOOL: A LIFE-OR-DEATH JUMP FROM YOUR COMFORT ZONE

After Ranger School, I wanted action! I was ready to live out every little boy's G.I. Joe fantasy, conquering with the rough and tough guys, the killers. So, I was excited to get my first assignment.

"You're going to teach trainees in Airborne School at Fort Benning in Georgia," the Army told me.

Talk about bursting my bubble! That sounded so dull and boring compared to the guts and glory of combat.

On the contrary, in my mind, this was not a prestigious assignment. I didn't want to do it. The instructors were not hardcore. They were regular. Having served in Iraq, I wanted to flex my mental and physical soldier swag on the battlefield. But soldiers don't call the shots; our superiors do. So, I had to swallow my pride and take this assignment.

The schedule was grueling. I had to wake up at 4:00 a.m., and I didn't get home until 6:00 p.m. Sometimes I was so tired, I would fall asleep in my uniform. I taught 12 classes per year from 2004 to 2006.

I didn't know it at the time, but this assignment was divinely orchestrated for me to help people. This is where motivational speaking first happened. It was all about me teaching an informal class by taking book knowledge and presenting it in a format that my students would learn, apply, and master. I did this by boiling tons of sometimes technical information down into the form of a conversation.

Guess what? This job was a huge blessing! I was the trainer, but this job was the ultimate training to prepare me for the future that I'm living right now as a motivational speaker.

I learned so much! First, I learned to trust that God is orchestrating everything that happens to us to prepare us to become our ultimate selves. Second, I learned to recognize that a treasure trove of knowledge and experience might be hidden under what looks like a disappointment or seemingly dull experience.

So, check this out: becoming a trainer in Airborne School was actually a crash course for me to learn how to speak in front of hundreds of people. It also boosted my confidence that I did, in fact, have something valuable to offer people and that I had the skills to help them succeed through leadership and advising students during Q&A sessions.

One day, I was leading 500 soldiers for an hour-long workout. It was 5:00 a.m., and they had to do whatever I said. At 26 years old, I was in great shape, and I had them running laps and doing push-ups.

"Now jumping jacks!" I ordered into my headphone-style microphone. I'd do the count, I'd do the rep, and they'd sign off with the number, with a call and response.

"Down!" I'd say. "One inch over the floor, up!"

"One!" the class said.

"Down, up!" I ordered.

"Two!" the class chanted.

People in the back were struggling and feeling sorry for themselves.

"You can do this!" I shouted. "Your body is telling you to quit, but you're better than that! You are not a quitter! Toughen your mind, and your body will follow!"

I could see my words registering in their minds, hearts, and souls, because they moved faster and harder. They responded to my call with louder voices. And the people who were struggling put more energy into the exercises.

Another time, I was leading hundreds of soldiers running on country roads at the crack of dawn. I called Army cadences, and they had to shout them back.

The energy inside me mirrored their energy. I was loving it!

The energy was so explosive, everybody seemed to work out harder. Afterwards, people came up to me and said, "You really helped me get through this! If it weren't for you, I don't know if I would have made it through this."

I was so excited, suddenly realizing that what was coming out of my mouth was inspiring people to push harder and be better.

Every time we worked out, which was every morning — the standard five-mile run — I discovered that the harder I was on them, with a combination of toughness and love, the students ran faster, with more enthusiasm.

"You're great for these students, man," said Command Sergeant Major Chris Lynch, my boss at the time. "Keep doing what you're doing." Then he showed me a stack of hundreds of critiques from students. "Look man, this whole stack of papers is coming back from your students, and they say you're great."

From there, I went on to teach other courses. The lesson here again is that God put me in a situation that I didn't particularly want, but it was His divine classroom to train me and show me how to become someone who can speak in front of hundreds, even thousands, to inspire them to do their best.

JUMPING OUT OF MY COMFORT ZONE — FROM AN AIRPLANE!

Airborne School was all about conquering fear. It shoved me out of my comfort zone, because I had to jump out of airplanes and helicopters, and teach students to do the same.

They started with ground exercises, followed by a week of jumping off a 34-foot tower simulating an aircraft. That's three stories high, and it's where most people have to conquer their fear of height. The students jumped off while hooked to cables — hundreds of times — to prepare for jumping out of helicopters and airplanes. I also taught them how to manipulate parachutes to function during jumps.

Throughout the course of this, I also taught Jumpmaster School and Pathfinder School, teaching nearly 15,000 people in 17 months. It was tough, and the graduation rate reflected that. Airborne School, for example, started with 500 students, but only 300 to 350 graduated.

Jumping out of an airplane is scary. So I used a lot of humor to motivate the students to do their best. And every Sunday, I led prayers with guys who were afraid about our jump the next day. They were feeling sorry for themselves and feeling weak. These men and women had been in agony for two weeks straight, training every day from 5:00 a.m. until 6:00 p.m. Then they had one day off, and they had to jump the next day.

"Let's gather around and pray," I said. "Lord, you know these young men and women are going to do something great tomorrow.

We pray for their safety and for them to have successful careers and successful jumps, and be safe and sound on graduation day."

As a Pathfinder Instructor, I taught hundreds of soldiers how to jump out of airplanes. After performing hundreds of jumps myself, this photo shows me helping a soldier exit a UH-60 Blackhawk helicopter 1,500 feet above Fort Benning, Georgia in 2008.

Prayer empowered them with courage and success during the jumps. At the same time, I discovered that the more I led people in prayer, the better my career became. Back then, you weren't supposed to talk about God. But I did, and was blessed with favor every time. I wasn't even a chaplain, but I was speaking divinity into people's lives. At first I was afraid to share my faith, but the more I did it, the better results we saw, and that encouraged me to do it more and more with no fear.

A jump is a life-or-death experience. The airplane is moving at 130 miles per hour. You're scanning the ground and calculating in your head when to jump so you can land on the designated spot.

"Go! Go! Go!" I shout to my students.

As you jump, all you can remember is what your instructor drilled into your head. You have to follow those instructions to a T, or you can die. Hitting the ground is rough, even when you do everything with perfect precision. Every time we had 500 people jumping in the unforgiving heat from 1,000 feet in the air, somebody always got hurt or knocked out or broke an arm or leg or multiple people passed out.

It's easy to panic when you're falling at 18 to 22 feet per second. It feels like the ground is coming up at you. I know this, because I did 92 jumps from helicopters and airplanes between 1996 and 2011. It hurts to land, because you're using muscles and fat, not bones, to break your fall.

Teaching Airborne School was one of the most rewarding experiences of my life. And it started off as something I didn't want to do! It pushed me way beyond the abilities I thought I had, and it boosted my faith in God's greater plan for our lives; it showed that He is always orchestrating our lives with new opportunities to learn, grow, and help people. The trick is to be obedient to His lessons, and put them to use in ways that benefit and inspire others.

Now I understand why I spent 20 years in the military, always pushing myself out of the easy place. I did not want to participate in easy operations. I always wanted to go to the toughest unit, not really understanding why at the time. I understand now, and I'm still doing it.

Now is your time to flee the easy place, and soar toward your greatest potential.

Be Unreasonable with Life

You have to learn to be unreasonable with life — by setting unreasonable goals. That's the only way you're going to learn how to find out what's inside.

For example, I want to celebrate my next birthday in Peru amongst the ancient and deeply spiritual ruins of Machu Picchu, which is known as the "Lost City of the Incas." It's one of the most spectacular and mysterious places in the world, and I want to go there. I don't speak the language. It's difficult to access the mountain-top structures for anyone, especially a double amputee on prosthetic legs.

I could kick back at a five-star resort with waiters catering to my every whim to celebrate. By the way, a birthday is always an extra special celebration for anyone who's survived a near-death experience. My prevailing thought is, "Thank you, Lord, for rescuing me from the valley of death and helping me soar into a whole new life." I also think of John 14:12, when Jesus tells us: "Verily, verily, I say unto you, He that believeth on me, the works that I do shall he do also; and greater *works* than these shall he do; because I go unto my Father."

If the miracle-working healer we know as Jesus says we can do greater works than he did, then we have to live up to his expectations! Jesus was the king of getting out of a comfort zone. He went into the desert alone to fast for 40 days. He fearlessly faced his enemies. He journeyed to new towns to spread the gospel, even though his adversaries despised him. But he was fueled by a higher purpose. What better example can we follow?

Taking a trip to Peru and believing that we can all do greater works than Jesus is being unreasonable with life. We are demanding more of ourselves than the average person can ever conceive. The reality is, nobody has to be average, even if you have an apparent setback such as losing your legs. Be unreasonable! Make demands on yourself and on God!

I say this because most of us ask for crumbs without knowing that the most decadent buffet is available for us to feast on — if only we ask. But we're too afraid, or we think too small to even realize that it exists.

Sadly, we're so used to asking for what we think we deserve. God is like, "You don't deserve anything. I'm giving you unreasonable every day. You stepped on 30 pounds of dynamite. Because you could do one thing unreasonably, you lived!" What I did unreasonably was believe in the face of death that I would survive. I called on God and trusted that He would bring me through. I kept acting like Master Sergeant Cedric King, giving orders from a stretcher, even though my legs had just been blown off. I was being unreasonable, and God rewarded me.

God doesn't reward mediocrity or small thinking. Ask for crumbs, you'll get them. In fact, a scripture says that those with the most will receive more and those with little will lose even that. It's all about using what you have to do better, to do more.

So, challenge God. Tell Him that you're ready to do those greater works. God works miracles. He likes to show out by doing the impossible. Not tending to menial tasks.

Dream big, ask big, make unreasonable demands on yourself and on God! Say something like: "I want to become a millionaire with my business." Or, "I want to find the person of my dreams and get married on a tropical island."

How about, "I want to lead a fundraising campaign to raise enough money for researchers to find a cure for the disease that claimed the life of someone I love." You could say, "I want to travel to a poor nation and open a hospital so women can give birth in sanitary conditions."

And you could ask God to show you how to invent a device that will transform the way we live, like Bill Gates and computers, or Thomas Edison and light bulbs, or Henry Ford and the assembly line for making cars. Think big, and make unreasonable demands for God to help you make it happen!

I have been doing this for years. That's how I, as a double amputee, am running marathons and always pushing myself to a bigger, badder challenge.

FINDING THE STRENGTH YOU DIDN'T KNOW YOU HAD

To achieve these big things in life, we need superhuman strength. My experience with hand cycling in the Walt Disney Marathon, which I described in Chapter 4 about Persevering Through the Pain, is another example of this.

As I sat at the starting line in my hand cycle, which is operated with gears that require using your arms to propel you across the 26.2 miles ahead, I feel like I'm throwing myself into the fire. I have no idea what I'm about to endure. Everybody around me is giving me a high five and saying things like, "Man, you got so much guts!" and I'm saying, "I've never sat in one of these! I have no clue."

But boy, was I about to get one. The gun went off, and about 30 wheelchair and hand cyclists took off like a drag race. I was the first person at the starting line, and the last to take off. I get maybe 100 yards down the road, and I'm thinking, *There's no way people can do this. I'm at 100 yards and I feel like my arms about to pop off my body!*

Would this be my breaking point or my Making Point? Well, I think you know me well enough by now to answer that question. But that sure didn't make it any easier! My mind was a tornado, whipped up by pride and all the motivational words that I have shared with thousands of people over the years since my injury. I could never encourage people to persevere through their own pain and triumph over their own life traumas, then turn around and quit something as high-profile and symbolic as this race.

So, I immersed in the workshop of my mind to manufacture some kind of messaging to provide mental strength and physical power to get through this seemingly impossible challenge. When you're thinking there's nothing you can do, that you have no capacity to make it, the truth is this — you can make it!

In this race, from miles one to five, I thought it was hopeless. My arms were on fire! And if you're not moving your arms, then the chair isn't rolling, unless you're going downhill. But just when you think it's impossible, you're reaching the Making Point. My body was protesting, but my mind said, *Let's find a way to transform this breaking point into a Making Point.*

Here's the formula:

1. Your mind says, "No way!" That's the NEGATIVE.

2. Identify that your obstacle is bigger than your belief. That's what makes the mind say no. Disagree with yourself. "My

mind says no, but something bigger than me says yes. And what's bigger than me is my belief. It's God. It's my desire to do something way beyond normal boundaries, that will show others that anything is possible, and will prove to myself that I can accomplish great things." That forces me to say, "Yes! Yes, I can do this!" That's the POSITIVE.

The bottom line is, when you put the negative with the positive, the outcome is the will to continue. Here's the formula:

NEGATIVE + POSITIVE = The will to continue.

You can also look at it like this: Negative + Changing Your Relationship to the Negative − The will to continue. So how can you do this? Trick yourself!

Remember how I flip my thoughts about things that seem terrible, into something that works to my advantage? Like when I asked, *What if my human legs were my obstacle, and God had to remove them in order for me to reach my greatest potential?*

That's a radical and innovative way to conquer an obstacle. So apply this same thinking to whatever problem you're confronting. For me, during the hand cycling race, I'm confronting the road, the distance, and the hills. So I have to change my relationship with the hill. I have to befriend it, even if that means slowing down. Doing this enables you to gain power over the obstacle. When we change our relationship with the enemy, the pain, the problem, we can befriend it. We draw power from it. It becomes our resource to blast past barriers and uplift other people in the process.

MARATHON MILES ARE A METAPHOR FOR LIFE

When I reach Mile 5, something happens that makes me start believing. Runners begin catching up to me. For the person in a wheelchair, the only running people are the five-minute milers. Regular runners are starting to catch me. To me — the super-fit Army Ranger who scored 300s on my PT tests — that's the heartbreak: seeing slow people catch me. All I can think is, "THERE IS NO WAY!"

I am overwhelmed by stinging disappointment. That's the negative. The positive is that it forces me to release my outcome. It made me surrender to the reality of the situation and find a new way to triumph.

No, I would not finish the race in a certain length of predetermined time. But I will finish the race! I have to let go of expectation. I have to stop thinking in terms of shoulda, woulda, coulda, and how things would be different if I had prepared better, or mastered this sport prior to registering for the race.

The reality is that I didn't, and I hadn't, so here I am, facing the consequences. Accepting the grim reality of the current circumstances helps me release the outcome.

When I stop saying, "You're supposed to be at Mile X by now," then I stop trying to control it. It is so freeing to release the expectation. When that happens, those miles start to come easier and easier, and my brain stops shouting, "THERE IS NO WAY!" Instead, I declare, "I can do this!" The ultimate goal is to finish — not to finish in a certain amount of time. Then the miles come easier. And I am grateful.

"Wow, thank you for another mile," I think while passing Mile 6, then Mile 8.

I've been in tough situations before where I wanted to quit marathons. Right now, the pain in my arms is tough, but I feel I can mentally muscle through it. The message is: you have to persist! Even when your mind says no.

"One push at a time," I tell myself.

Push, Rest, Push, Rest.

This requires acute mental focus.

Whatever you're facing, find your *one* thing at a time.

Taking one step at a time.

Losing one pound at a time.

Doing one squat at a time.

Sealing one new business deal at a time.

Writing one sentence at a time.

This chapter is all about knowing your strength. This story is all about believing that you can find the strength you didn't know you had! And that will serve as proof the next time around.

You can dominate anything with one push at a time. If you can do one step at a time, you can finish the journey. The problem is, we think we're supposed to conquer things 10 at a time or 20 at a time, just like the person next to us might be doing. But that causes disappointment.

When you compare, you despair.

But when you find your own rhythm — *Push, Rest, Push, Rest* — you find your groove. You discover what has your identity on it. One push. One rest. One push. One rest. That's where I am, over the course of 26.2 miles. Thankfully, hills come along to help; after the climb, I'm rewarded with a downhill glide. This is tough! At one point, it hurts so bad, I take my hand off the wheel, and roll backwards! Still, I am determined to finish this race. The sun sets. Even though it's Florida, it's cold — 42 degrees. But I find patience with myself. So I hit the brakes and rest, then push, while runners speed past. They want to help.

And I want to find the lesson here. I need to summon understanding from deep within myself to transform this incredible challenge into a metaphor for life that I can share with you. I feel a jolt of excitement at the idea of finishing, and adding this seemingly impossible accomplishment to my list of victories.

Apply this idea to anything in your life, because marathons are a powerful metaphor for achieving anything. I cannot stress this enough. We live in a country where we're constantly bombarded by messages that we need X amount of money, a luxury car, a house with a certain number of square feet, the right jewelry, the best job title, prestigious degrees, and designer watches. But when you release that pressure, that measure by external factors, and find your own pace, magic happens. You relax. And you win your own race, on your own time.

BOSTON IN A WHEELCHAIR: NO GLOVES, BUT LOTS OF GLORY

My legs have been so battered from running marathons in my prosthetics that I decided to use a wheelchair to compete in the 2017 Boston Marathon. You'd think I would have learned my lesson from prior experiences about training and preparing, but here again, I am embarking on a very difficult endurance challenge. This time, however, that is not the problem.

My racing wheelchair was shipped to Boston, along with my helmet and special gloves. The wheelchair and helmet arrive. The gloves — which were custom-made and took four-to-six weeks to be sent to my home — do not show up. And you cannot use a racing wheelchair without heavy-duty gloves, because you literally "punch" the wheels to make them turn as fast as possible. Not using gloves will destroy your hands.

"We have to make a pair of gloves!" I tell Kenya at 4:00 p.m. on Sunday in Boston. The police are starting to barricade the streets to prepare for the race, which starts in 13 hours. Kenya and I Uber all over town, looking for stores that might sell gloves. Finally, we find the only athletic store open on Sunday night in Boston. The employees in the shoe store are about to close. They're packing up stuff, and lowering the gate to block people from coming in, when I hobble in on prosthetics and say,

"Let me see the biggest shoes that you guys have."

We find size 15 Adidas. It's an old, cheap pair. We take the shoes to the hotel, along with knives, pieces of plastic, tape, fabric, straps, and Velcro. And, get this, I make a pair of racing gloves out of gym shoes!

The next morning, I'm at the starting line with all the guys who are wearing the coolest shades and top gear from fancy sponsors. They look like gladiators. As the gun fires, I'm still trying to figure out how to turn on my iPod and plug up my music. Others bolt like they have motors hooked up to their wheelchairs. They're out of sight after a minute. Luckily, the course starts on a downhill. Meanwhile, I'm still trying to work with these homemade gloves. It's almost like a waste of time because they're slipping off my hands.

I feel stupid, trying to wave at people with a gym shoe! My playlist is all messed up. Then I hit my first hill with the shoe-gloves and they're not working. I'm like, "What is the use?"

Then I realize, THIS IS LIFE. And I just keep going.

Between Mile 1 and Mile 2, I'm saying, *There's no way*. Except, I have the unique fortune to reflect on past obstacles. Well, if I figured it out that time, and that other time, too, and was able to stay in the fire a little bit longer, then I tell myself that I can make it to Mile 2, catch a couple down hills, and see how that goes.

It's exciting to realize that I'm already far ahead of my previous three Boston marathons as far as time milestones. To me, that's already a win.

I'm here already! If I were running, I wouldn't even be there right now. That becomes my motivation. The gloves are a sore spot, but because I have a clock and figured out my playlist, my excitement rescues my thoughts from despairing over things not being perfect. And when the hills show up to teach me more lessons, I am too far to quit.

The hills get steep. I become so overwhelmed with fatigue, that I can barely push. All I can think about is getting to a point where it will be easier. I want to rush through the "now" and get to the "next" where it won't hurt so much. But wishing for something other than what you have at that moment is what makes you tired. Like when you're wishing you were at the top of the hill or at the finish line, or wanting the sunny day to be here when it's raining. We always want to jump to the thing that makes it easy.

What if we tried relaxing in the difficulty, in the place where we don't want to be? What if you just surrender to the fact that you are at the steep part of the hill, and it's mentally and physically grueling? What if you stopped wasting energy on wishing you had a different job, or a more loving spouse, or a faster car, or a life like the glory days of your past, or a vacation on the beach? What if you just stay right there, right now, and notice everything about it, good and bad?

This idea crystallizes on those hills. It happens after Mile 16, when my focus is on my fatigue. Suddenly I stop obsessing about, "When am I going to get my rest break?" Instead, I become more energized by closing my eyes, with my head down, feeling everything about this exact moment.

Focus on this push. Focus on this moment. Grind out this moment. Get in this fight.

As I begin to feel better, I force myself to forget about how close I am to the top of the hill. I tell myself, *Be right here, right now. Be on this push. Be on this push. Not at the top of the hill. Right here, right now. You're at the steep part of the hill.*

Bam! It gets easier...

I win the fight against myself. I use my breaking point as another Making Point to prove that resilience and perseverance are rewarded by personal fulfillment, a medal at the finish line, and the gift of showing other people that they, too, can do what they think is impossible.

While I don't defeat any elite wheelchair racers, I beat Cedric's last race time. Like Kenya says, when you compare, you despair. So, I don't compare my time to others. I compare it to myself. And that's exciting! I beat my previous best! Set your own barometer. Race against yourself. The rewards are so much more gratifying. And in doing so, you set an example for others to follow.

Amazingly, I do my fastest marathon time ever at 3:07 — with broken parts! By comparison, I did the Florida wheelchair marathon in 4:24. Boston is a far harder course. That's why I know that whatever looks impossible comes into your life to help you see the treasures that are already buried inside you. When things look bad, that means the blessings are about to hit.

This time, the Boston Marathon taught me so much. First, embrace the moment where everything is about to break. The best comes out of you when you're short-handed. When you don't have the resources. When everybody is against you. When all the people and all the circumstances are at their worst, you become at your best. These are not easy lessons.

In this case, the best came out when I had no gloves. When you make a way out of *no way*, you win the fight against yourself. You stick with it until something comes along and allows you to persist when you feel like quitting.

There Is No Making Point Without God

Throughout these challenges and lessons, I know one thing for sure: there is no Making Point without God. If you're an atheist, this book is not for you. Because my message only works through the lens of faith. There is no Making Point without God because God sends the obstacle to make you. God knows exactly how we are built. He knows what challenges to throw in our paths. He wanted me to learn new things in Boston this time. So He tossed in the desperation that sparked the innovation to make my own gloves, as an extra test of my ability to make a way out of no way.

He knows exactly how much you can take. God knows that the moment you persevere through pain and difficulty is the exact second that you see the light, deepen your faith, and charge forward more aggressively to execute the divine life mission that He has assigned to you. So be an eager student, especially when times get tough, and feel grateful that God is showing you how to draw on His supernatural power to achieve anything, anytime, anywhere. All you have to do is believe that your human breaking point is actually your spiritual Making Point.

Your Life Is A Battle Against The Resistance. Win!
When I was on duty in the Middle East, we were always fighting
against the resistance. We had to execute a mission to stop them, and
we had to defend ourselves from their attacks.

Life is the same. Every day, we are fighting the resistance of forces
that are attempting to hold us back from our best lives. Bad emotions
like fear, worry, doubt, insecurity, and sadness can be the resistance.
Situations such as an accident, a bankruptcy, death of a loved one, job
loss, foreclosure, illness, and injuries can be the resistance. And bad
habits like being lazy, procrastinating, staying on the couch instead
of going to the gym, eating junk food, gossiping, failing to plan, and
blowing your money on things you don't need — these can all be the
resistance as well.

If you don't fight back, you will lose, and suffer all kinds of
consequences.

So, you have to fight back! You deserve better!

But it takes action. You can't get complacent. On the battlefield,
that's the path to injury and death. When you let your guard down
or stop fighting altogether, you become a sitting duck for your enemies. In civilian life, your enemies come in too many forms to count.
So, you need to look at your life — your personal battlefield — and
devise a strategy to defeat your enemies.

Life gives you the opportunity to be an Army Ranger every day.
I've said it before, but just to remind you, that's the toughest soldier
you can become. What if you applied that same mindset to your life?
That you are undefeatable, and that you can obliterate any obstacles
that your enemies try to put in your way of being your best self and
making your dreams come true.

The problem? You became an Army Ranger for a reason. Joining the military is way, far out of your comfort zone. In fact, it's human nature to want to nestle into our comfort zones and stay there. That could be a relationship, a job, a situation, an unhealthy weight, the sofa, you name it. But your comfort zone is actually a trap that will choke the life out of your dreams. I want to help you escape!

How-To Exercises

Describe your comfort zones, where you feel safe and cozy and content to stay there. Then explain why that comfort zone is hurting you rather than helping you. Finally, write the action required to escape that comfort zone to create a better you and a better life.

Comfort Zone #1

_____

_____

_____

_____

How is it helping me?

_____

_____

_____

_____

How is it hurting me?

_____

_____

_____

_____

What ACTION can I take to escape this comfort zone to achieve a goal and be a better me?

_____

_____

_____

_____

Comfort Zone #2

_____

_____

_____

_____

How is it helping me?

_____

_____

_____

_____

How is it hurting me?

_____

_____

_____

_____

What ACTION can I take to escape this comfort zone to achieve a goal and be a better me?

_____

_____

_____

_____

Comfort Zone #3

_____

_____

_____

_____

How is it helping me?

_____

_____

_____

_____

How is it hurting me?

_____

_____

_____

_____

What ACTION can I take to escape this comfort zone to achieve a goal and be a better me?

_____

_____

_____

_____

Comfort Zone #4

_____

_____

_____

_____

How is it helping me?

_____

_____

_____

_____

How is it hurting me?

_____

_____

_____

_____

What ACTION can I take to escape this comfort zone to achieve a goal and be a better me?

_____

_____

_____

_____

Imagine that your life is a battlefield and you are an Army Ranger fighting all resistance that blocks you from living your best life. Describe those obstacles and your battle plan to defeat them. You can also write about each area of your life as a battlefield, such as your relationships, your job, your home, and problematic situations.

_____

_____

_____

_____

Reflect on moments when you realized you were stronger than you thought.

_____

_____

_____

_____

What are you deeply passionate about?

_____

_____

_____

What would it take to fulfill your dreams or visions for your future?

_____

_____

_____

Write down steps to get from here to there.

_____

_____

_____

_____

What risks would you be willing to take to succeed?

_____

_____

_____

_____

What would be your biggest fear for taking the first step?

_____

_____

_____

_____

9

Inspiring by Example

SILENCE THE INNER CRITIC BY WRITING A NEW STORY FOR YOUR LIFE

I've always wanted to be a public speaker. But how can you speak words of inspiration to strangers, if the voice inside your head is shouting words of defeat and doom to discourage you? How can you achieve any goal — losing weight, going back to school, opening a business, improving your relationships, getting a better job, anything — if you're telling yourself that you can't do it?

You have to silence your inner critic. You have to shut down that voice in your head that's announcing what you can't do, and telling you what's impossible. Then you have to blast a mental broadcast to yourself that you can do anything you want. You have to convince yourself in your mind that anything is possible. I'm a walking, talking testimony of that.

But growing up, I had plenty of reasons to never believe in myself. Financial struggles. Bullies. Bad grades. A dad who wasn't around consistently. Then, after my accident, I could have allowed the physical and emotional pain, as well as the trauma of losing my legs and my career as a soldier, to push me down into a dark place. I could have abandoned my dream of running, after doctors discouraged it. I could have allowed my inner critic to look at my circumstances and convince me that my future would be miserable. Maybe not even worth living.

But I forced my inner critic to shut up. I silenced that negative voice. Better yet, I replaced that self-critical soundtrack with a can-do spirit that has enabled me to rise up to become the best Cedric ever, and inspire people from stages across America and the world.

Here's the bottom line: I realized that every one of us is the editor-in-chief of our own personal newspaper. The newsroom is inside our heads, and we have the power to decide what stories to cover for that day. Then we have the ability to write the headlines, do the researching and reporting to compile the information to substantiate the headlines, then compose the story.

The best part is this: we get to announce the story to the world. We can publish it in bold, black and white print. We have the ability to blast it out like our own personal broadcast. With the internet, we can publish a blog and broadcast videos all around the planet.

Come up with great story ideas, gather the information you need, and share the breaking news. You'll get great ratings from yourself and every person who sees and hears your reports. Now, guess who and what the lead story is, every day of your life?

YOU! Yes, you, and everything you're doing!

As the editor-in-chief of *You News*, you have to make a lot of decisions every day. It all starts with intention. What is your goal? Your goal is to make a powerful impact with the stories that you print for public consumption. Here's the problem: most of us have spent our entire lives running a newspaper inside our heads that comes up with the most negative news we can compose about ourselves:

I can't do that. I'd rather stay in this job and be miserable than risk following my dreams, because if I fail, my life will be ruined. I'll never lose weight; every time I've tried, I've failed. My marriage is doomed; there's nothing I can do to improve it. I can't afford to go back to school; I have to stay in this dead-end job to pay my bills. If I try to open my own business, nobody will buy my products or use my services.

I can't...

That's impossible...

I'll never...

I'm just a regular person. I can't do anything exceptional.

Yes, you can! You can do anything your heart desires! I've got news for you: everybody has something inside that is extraordinary and screaming to be released. We've been hypnotized to believe that it's better and safer to be one of the group, someone who just goes along to get along, without taking risks. There is no safety in that. There is no life in that!

I meet a lot of people who say, "I don't know if I'm created to be exceptional. I've always been normal. I just want to collect my check, spend weekends with my family, and go back to work on Monday. I don't want any responsibility."

Here's what I tell them: "You're lying to yourself! You've bought into a group mentality that encourages mediocrity over achievement. You've sold yourself that lie. But you have the power to write a new story for yourself and your life."

You have the ability to serve as the most powerful propaganda machine you can imagine — because you are your own high-powered publicist! You can be a public relations phenomenon!

You just need the right message. Unfortunately, most of us are promoting the wrong messages. They are bogged down with anger, doubt, frustration, fear, failure, insecurity, and laziness.

But listen, I'm here to tell you, when you take control of that newspaper outlet inside your head, you can transform yourself and the world around you! When we start listening to that voice inside that says, "You are created for much more than this," we begin to see opportunities arise. We start to see our paths lead us in a different direction.

Since our brains push our bodies, we have to think differently, in order to live differently. The problem is, our brains are full of noise. The noise of pain, fatigue, and all the negative things I mentioned above.

For me, the noise was, *I don't want to do it anymore.* The pain, the surgeries, the struggles, the fear, the questioning. Things in my life didn't start changing until I learned how to shut down my negative propaganda machine and instead produce a daily internal newscast of encouragement, hope, and faith that I could do anything.

I got the good news headlines up and running in *The Cedric Daily Post* after I remembered how I had mastered the art of keeping a positive news ticker streaming in my head as an Army Ranger. Here's an example. In the Army, the morning exercise included a six-mile run with your squad, your platoon. Your sergeant tells you to run out three miles as a group, then turn around and run three miles back. The first person to run back first, wins — and doesn't have to do push-ups.

I always wanted to be first. I didn't want anyone to beat me. I didn't want to be among the rest of the gang. It didn't matter how bad it hurt to be first. I would just push myself to be first. I yearned to be elite. At the top. A fire was burning inside me to be the best. So, as the editor-in-chief of my own newspaper, I wrote this headline: *I Know I'm Elite and I'm Willing to Push Past the Pain of the Noise.* Then I focused on that story, and did everything necessary to broadcast it to myself and to the world. But sometimes it was really hard to hear my own report over the deafening noise inside my head.

This hill is steep!

My lungs feel like they're on fire!

I am so fatigued!

Fortunately, the voice of "I want to be first" was always louder. In fact, I cranked the volume. Amplified it in my mind. And it became HYPNOTIC. All I had to do was outrun the fastest guy and be first, then it was worth being tired. It was worth the pain. Pain that was only temporary. Whereas, the pride of being first would last for a lifetime.

"Cedric," I asked myself during the toughest moments, "do you settle for being second and forgotten about, or being first and always being remembered?"

It was an easy decision. I never want to be a normal, regular guy. Something inside me deserves to be outstanding. Something inside YOU deserves to be outstanding. When you really start to believe that, you'll begin to push yourself.

The bad news is that settling for mediocrity is human nature. It's the path of least resistance. The Army taught me that. If I pour water on top of a hill, it will flow downhill along the easiest route.

I learned this the hard way during my first attempt at Ranger School, when I had to take the Land Navigation Test. I had already passed infantry training, but being out in the rugged wilderness during the wintertime in Washington state was a much more difficult experience. That's why Army Rangers are elite; we are trained in extreme conditions.

This particular test of my speed, strength, and navigational abilities required me to traverse rugged terrain using only the equipment provided by the Army: old instruments, compasses, maps, and protractors. This was before GPS, when people had to navigate environments with these tools that seem primitive by today's high-tech standards. Why? They had to get to the battlefield undetected, using only compasses and maps. Every step of the way, challenges test your will. Vines, trees, bushes, lakes, and shrubs can throw you off path in the forest.

The Bible says in 2 Corinthians 5:7 that "we walk by faith, not by sight."

Well, humans rely on sight, and when you're under duress, it's easy to abandon faith and look for the easiest, quickest route from point A to point B. That's what I did. Even though I knew that nighttime navigation was most accurate when you rely on your Army instruments. That's the best way to go straight to your destination and pass the test.

The problem? It was winter, and a lake stood between me and my destination. The compass told me to cross the lake. I was tired, hungry, and cold. I didn't want to get wet, or risk my life crossing an icy lake without a boat or a life jacket. The bottom line was that I didn't trust the compass, because my physical and mental discomfort skewed my judgement.

Sometimes when you're tired, your compass will say you have to go north to reach your destination. But that's the difficult route. The path of least resistance will take you downhill in a southwest direction. If you allow fatigue and doubt to guide you that way, it will steer you off course. You'll get lost.

Well, on this fateful night, I wanted to follow the path of least resistance. And I got lost. My compass told me to cross the lake, straight through the water! I had no idea how deep the water was, due to melted snow and rainfall. Crossing a lake at night with no boat sounds life-threatening and impossible. That was the point; the course was designed to test your will, your courage, your physical fitness. If your will is strong enough, you ignore the obstacle.

While this was happening, my personal newspaper was blaring the wrong headline: CEDRIC TAKES THE EASY WAY. My breaking news was announcing: "This test is too hard! I can't do this the way they told me to do it. I'll die if I try to swim through an ice-cold lake! This is impossible! Forget this compass, I'm going to walk around and make it. My way is better!"

So I went around the lake, through thick vegetation, and got off course. Over time, map data changes. Vegetation grows and shrinks. I walked through it.

Little did I realize, that I was actually avoiding the obstacle of the lake, and that by trudging through it, I would triumph over the challenge, and pass the test. In hindsight, it was a great learning experience.

Sometimes, the obstacle is the co-worker. Or the health crisis. The financial problems. The threat of divorce. The accident. These dilemmas raise the question: "Will I face the obstacle head-on, or will I try to go around it?"

I learned that avoidance can get you into even greater trouble. Because I failed the Land Navigation Test. And I flunked Ranger School.

On my third attempt, I passed Army Ranger School in April 2004. I am in the second row down, the fourth soldier in from the right. We had just returned from the Florida swamps to Georgia, where we bathed for the first time in two months. © US Army.

BEST RANGER 2011 – Canoeing against the current on the Oochie Creek River with Brett Graves during the Best Ranger Competition at Fort Benning, Georgia was tough. We didn't win, but we were among the 20 finishers out of the 50 teams that started in this elite competition. © Army Times.

How To Write Happier Headlines For Yourself

You don't have to interview anyone to do this. You don't need to do any research. You already have the information inside you. It's called belief in yourself. It's called a positive outlook. A more upbeat attitude. And action. As the editor-in-chief of your own newspaper outlet, all you have to do is crank out new headlines, and take action on them.

This is the secret to how I changed my way of thinking, backed it up with action, and saw positive results in my life. It's very simple.

Number one is a repeat: start by doing what we say we're going to do.

For me, that's tough, because I say a lot of stuff. But when I speak about the things I'm very passionate about, I do them to the best of my ability. You have to be excellent in word and deed. Unfortunately, it's easy to say you're going to do a long list of grandiose things — but never follow through. That leaves you with zero credibility, because people will stop believing what you say.

I remember telling people I was going to run a marathon. That I was going to go to Ranger School. That I'd be the best in my company, and have a better shooting score than anyone. I wasn't bragging. I just knew what I wanted. I said it, then I took action and walked toward it. I made it happen. And when I did what I said I was going to do, I was blessed with favor. Good things happened.

That inspired me to do everything with excellence.

So how can you draw the courage, strength, and fortitude from within yourself to do that?

You don't need a guru. You are the guru of yourself. You don't have to spend money on a coach, or a seminar, or a class. All you have to do is spend time with yourself. Finding your Making Point is an inside job. You need to sit down. Just be quiet for a little while. Practice mindfulness. Sit down and listen to the voice inside.

Just like when you meet someone new, and you go on a date with him or her, you want to have long talks and learn everything about this fascinating new person. What's so exciting about that process is that the other person is probably going to say all kinds of really nice things to you that make you feel like the king or queen of the world. You're floating on air, and feel like you can do anything.

What if you could talk to yourself the same way?

Now is the time to fall in love with yourself. Just sit quietly alone, and think about who you are and how you can talk to your best version of yourself. I keep an "I love me" notebook where I write notes to myself.

This warrants repetition a million times. Unfortunately, other people, our devices, 24-hour news, and a whole host of other stuff, all become this noisy chorus of life that shouts down our inner voice. It deafens us to our intuition.

Just look around at people who are doing what you dream about doing. That's a message, an affirmation, that a better life, a better you, is yours for the taking. When you see greatness outside you, it speaks to micro greatness inside you. It's a supernatural message. And that little mirror of inspiration can get bigger and bigger.

Use Words To Create What You Want

When you silence your inner critic, you open the doors to a life that's as great as your imagination can fathom. Proverbs 18:21 says, "Death and life are in the power of the tongue: and they that love it shall eat the fruit thereof."

That means: what you say can give life to your dreams. It also warns that your words can kill your dreams.

So only speak what you want! Declare: "I can be and do anything I want. I have the power to decide what I want, and to become it. I can do it!"

Unfortunately, your inner critic is going to spew words of death over everything. When you see your dream car whiz past, it will say, "You could never afford that car. Forget about it!" When you see a mansion, it will tell you, "That's way out of reach for you in this lifetime." When you walk past a beautiful woman or a handsome man, your inner critic will say, "You don't deserve someone like that."

If you allow your tongue to form over those words, you are creating doom. But when you use the power of your tongue to declare that you can and will have all of the above, you are one step closer to getting it all.

I want to be an Army Ranger.

I want to run marathons.

I want to drive my dream car.

I want to live in a beautiful home.

I declared it all. I wrote about it in my dream book. I put it on my vision boards. I put the car of my dreams as the screensaver on my computer.

I spoke it. I took action. And now I have achieved everything that I've said I would do, be, and get. Every day, I declare new goals, and work hard to achieve them.

How can you do this? Start speaking where you are. Just ask yourself, "What do I want out of life? Where do I want to go? What do I want to do?"

You may say you want a particular house. Then your inner critic will say, "I don't have that house." I'm here to tell you that yes, you do have that house. It just does not exist in the physical form. But it's real in the spiritual form. You have the power to speak it into existence!

Be patient, and remember Hebrews 11:1: "Now faith is the substance of things hoped for, the evidence of things not seen."

Know that it takes time to get there. Khieda and I used to drive around fancy neighborhoods in an old, beat-up Nissan. The muffler was about to fall off. It was so embarrassing.

"One day we're going to live in a gated neighborhood like this," I told her.

She didn't believe me. But I knew it. My physical eye was resonating with something inside my heart. That happens with all of us every day. That's why I know that the first step is to ask, "What do you want? Where do you want to live? What do you want to do?"

When you ask yourself these questions, listen to the answers. When they come, investigate them with curiosity. Look them up online. Find a magazine and cut out pictures of the house, the car, the dream job, the vacation, the people who look happy and peaceful. Then make a dream board. Post up the pictures of what you want in a place that you'll see every day.

I did this in 2006, and I have exactly what I declared I wanted — only better. That includes the car, the house, and the career. I never saw the amputation coming, but I saw everything else. I wrote in my journal that I wanted to be a world-renowned speaker and a best-selling author. And that's what I'm experiencing this very moment. I wrote that as a motivational speaker, or as I believe myself to be — a spiritual fitness trainer — I could command a certain amount. That happened. As I have worked to continuously perfect my craft, that amount has grown and exceeded my original declaration.

When I started to receive everything I asked for — and more — I realized that I was dreaming too small!

At the time in 2006 that I was writing about everything I wanted, I had two legs, but I was very dissatisfied with America's spiritual health during President George W. Bush's administration.

"I want to be president!" I declared, because I believed that I could fix everything that was wrong with the United States at the time. I wanted to steer our country in a better direction. Then I broadcast the wrong headline to myself. I was like, "Man, there's no way a black guy would be president."

Little did I know that just a few years later, President Barack Obama would get elected and prove me wrong. He gave me the "audacity of hope." That's what he named his 2006 book, *The Audacity of Hope: Thoughts on Reclaiming the American Dream.*

We all need to reclaim our dreams that have been trampled by life circumstances. Instead of doubting your ability to have and do everything you desire, declare, "Yes! I will have that."

Then — this step is very important — don't worry about "how" it will happen. If you're truly destined for something, God already has a plan for it.

Our custom-built home is an example of that. It's located in a beautiful neighborhood, and was designed and built with every convenience for a double amputee.

At the dedication ceremony, I spoke at a podium in front of our new home under a bright blue sky. As I thanked everyone involved in creating this house for me and my family, my voice cracked with emotion. Though I never could have imagined the amazing "how" of receiving our dream home, God already had it figured out. All I did was say, "Yes I will have it," and I never questioned how.

For most of us, our biggest detriment is asking, "How will I have it?" We stress over how it will happen so much until we "how" ourselves right out of our blessings. We "how" ourselves out of that grace and mercy that's already got our name on it. What do we do?

Our dream house.

How *this*? How *that*?

How steals the traction of *when* the blessing is coming. *When* and *how* create doubt in our minds. If you see the *how* on getting a better job, improving the marriage, winning the prize, or moving to a new city, those two words will immediately kill the inspiration and enthusiasm.

Here's another example: I don't get how it's going to happen, but I am going to be on Oprah. Yes, we're going to Super Soul Sunday. It will happen. I don't know *how*. It doesn't matter how. The truth is, I don't care how.

I simply say, "Yes, I will do that. I will be a wheelchair racer next year. I didn't know how. I'm going to finish Boston next year, and I'm going to be good at it."

I said it. I believed it. I didn't question how. I simply released it up to the heavens for God to make it happen. And He did.

SPEAKING INSPIRATION TO THOSE WHO NEED IT MOST

Becoming a public speaker was natural for me because I've always been a talker. But I never imagined that God would exchange my legs for the gift of my career as a motivational speaker. The accident gave me this new story, this new struggle, that provides powerful metaphors every single day that I can use to inspire people in my speeches.

I started doing that in the hospital, before I even had prosthetic legs. I would just go from room to room, talking with soldiers who'd been injured. Some of them were in terrible pain. Or they were depressed and suffering from anxiety. Some had Post Traumatic Stress Disorder. Others were angry about their loss of body parts, mobility, and life as they knew it. All I wanted to do was make people feel better. That desire was the same feeling that had made me, as a kid, give away all our food to other kids if they were hungry.

So now, I realized that by telling my story, and seeing the blessing in the burden of pain and change, I hoped to cheer people up and help them see that their lives were not over. They were just different. I continued to do this when I was an outpatient, and I remember visiting a soldier named Jason. He was injured in October of 2013, and his leg amputations were exactly like mine, except I have a left knee and he has a right knee. When I visited him, his parents were in the room. They were so sad.

"Yo, man, it's gonna get better," I told Jason, who at times was in and out of consciousness during my many visits. So, I assured his parents, "Just believe me. It's not what it looks like. It will get better." Over time, his mom really started feeling better.

I talked with a lot of amputees when I was at the hospital, and I just didn't want them to think that their lives were done or that they could not re-invent themselves. As I did this, God gave me the strength to keep a positive spirit despite the reality that I had lost my legs and was enduring excruciating pain all the time. Keeping a smile on my face wasn't even a conscious decision. If it had been, I would have failed. It was God Almighty. My ability to stay strong came from prayers, faith, and God's grace. I can't explain it any other way, because it could not have been just me.

"We're in awe of you," Secretary Carter and his wife, Stephanie, told me when they saw how I was encouraging older soldiers to stay strong. "You're so upbeat, and you're going to surgery tomorrow. How is that possible?"

"I'm just being me," I answered. "I'm not trying to be somebody inspirational."

That moment with them was a real revelation. Sometimes it takes another person's observation and comments to serve as a mirror for you to see who you really are. I realized that having a good attitude can truly determine how people view life. That moment with the Carters, and the connection we formed, began my understanding of how this injury could help other people.

"Wow, Cedric," I told myself, "you can influence the outcomes of other people because they get it when you smile. You didn't allow it to get you down. Your smiling gives them hope that nothing is above life. No matter how tough things are, it's still not above putting a smile on your face and living through it."

Stephanie Carter described me this way: "He's a sunny, active, driven, and kind person to be around. Adversity reveals character. His character was always one of searching for the good in things and not allowing trying times to knock him down. When he speaks, I know he has just made everyone in the room feel better. So, I told him, if he could go ahead and get through this time in his life and spread his positivity to others, I didn't think there was anything he couldn't do. I felt immediately that that was his calling."

Giving My First Speech Outside The Hospital

My first official speech was at the wedding of First Lt. Jake Gregory Kohlman and his new wife, Melissa Ann Oliver, a teacher. After they married on November 10, 2012, in a big wedding at Nationals Park, the baseball stadium in Washington, DC, I had the honor of speaking about life and love before them, their guests, and Khieda.

"We asked Cedric to say something, which he did, and everyone was very touched," Jake recalls. "He talked about commitments. He'd just been through some terrible stuff and couldn't have done it without Khieda. He also talked about the importance of having a life partner, as well as appreciating the value of the positive and sometimes the negative times in life. King is a natural speaker. These injuries didn't break him out of his shell. He was always an opinionated, loud person. His injuries for all intents and purposes should have killed him, if not for [Doc] Keller and the platoon. But he has always been relentlessly positive. He likes talking to people. Loves mentoring. Still stayed in touch with everyone from our platoon. Talks to famous people the same way he talks to a Sergeant E5 in the Army who is not famous. King treats everyone well, which is admirable. On top of that, running marathons requires a level of dedication and mental perseverance that is unfathomable to me."

What I learned by speaking at Jake's wedding was this: *All I had to do was be me. Nothing else.* At the wedding, I was sitting in a motorized wheelchair and I thought, "Just be the real Cedric." I couldn't hide behind anything. I felt almost naked. I was wearing shorts, and my bandaged legs were exposed. I was extremely vulnerable. And when you're most vulnerable, you're most powerful. People want real.

Being unable to hide behind the fact that I don't have legs is the quickest way to be vulnerable. I go straight to being the real Cedric. So, I wear shorts. Because people get inspired by the real you.

What can you do daily to be vulnerable, and therefore, real?

Mockery Can Push You Out Of Mediocrity

Years before Jake's wedding, I gave a speech early in my career, and it was bad.

But it was a powerful experience, because it taught me about major motivators in my life: the words "No" and "You can't." Say those words to me, and I guarantee, my answer will be "Yes, I can!" I'll say it, and I'll do it.

So now when I give a speech, I tell my story first. Then I talk about how the docs told me it wasn't possible to run 10 miles within a year of my injury. I explain that I couldn't control the doctors. But I could control how I responded. Instead of using their discouragement as an excuse, I said, "Look, I'm not a normal guy. I can do it!"

Now, the most powerful encouragement you can give me is to say, "That's impossible," or "I don't believe you can do that." Skepticism from naysayers has been the common denominator for all of my greatest accomplishments.

During my early years with the Army, I spoke at a graduation. Nervousness pulsed through me as I approached the podium, then gave the speech. I flopped! Still, one lady saw my potential. She walked up and said, "You're pretty good at this." She provided what most people seek as affirmation to pursue their dreams. However, the opposite is really what you need. And my buddies provided it with ridicule:

"Give it up!" they taunted.

"Man, you're crazy!" they said.

Their criticism flipped my "I-can-do-this switch" on full blast. It also convinced me that public speaking was my destiny, because their ridicule triggered my desire to do it even more. They had no idea that they were actually fueling my fire to accomplish something that looked impossible to them. I needed that resistance, that push-back, that laughter. It's the guard at the door to your dreams, warning, "Don't take another step. I'm here to make sure you can't come inside."

That makes me want to push that door open to get the valuable prize behind it. That won't happen if I allow the door to slam shut, or if I run away in fear or shame without trying to open it.

So, when people laugh, or degrade you, especially about your heart's desire, then know that you're on your path to your destiny.

Name any great person, and I guarantee he or she endured ridicule, naysayers, and even injustice. Michael Jordan. Dr. Martin Luther King, Jr. Mahatma Gandhi. Nelson Mandela.

Every great person followed the same blueprint. The difference between them and others is that average people allow the resistance to push them into mediocrity. The great ones use the resistance to push themselves forward. Remember this: pain *pushes* you — and purpose *pulls* you — into things you never would have done before.

So, the next time something tries to discourage you from reaching your goals and making your dreams come true, transform that discouragement into encouragement. Perception is reality, and when you perceive success in every situation, especially those that look like failure, you are fueling your quest to make good things happen for yourself and others.

I am so grateful to all the people who have helped me bring these messages to stages across America. Back in the early days, two people were especially helpful: Carolina Panthers Coach Ron Rivera, and National Association of Minority Automotive Dealers President Damon Lester.

A Boomerang of Inspiration with my Favorite Football Team

Sometimes you can go after something you really want, and when you get it, you realize that the experience has inspired an endless cycle of giving and receiving that you never imagined before it happened.

That's my story with the Carolina Panthers football team. I've always been a huge fan.

Shortly after I came out of the coma and surgery, I wanted to visit the Panthers, who were preparing to play the Washington Redskins.

My commanding officer had a connection with one of the coaches, and he helped me get a meeting with Panthers Head Coach Ron Rivera.

"Right away, I can tell this guy has a different outlook on life," Coach Rivera said during an interview for this book. "He was telling me about his injury, and an experience he had in Walter Reed."

That experience that I shared with Coach Rivera was about the day when a doc put me in a wheelchair and wheeled me out to the lobby of a recreation area.

"Now Sergeant King, over there," the doc said, "those are the people who are waiting to die." Then the doc pointed to a group of people on the other side of the room.

"Over here are the people who want to live," he said. "What do you want?"

I took one look and gunned toward those who wanted to live.

As I shared the rest of my story, Coach Rivera was very impressed, and invited me to speak to his team the night before the Redskins game on November 4, 2012.

Here is Coach Rivera's account of that meeting and how we became friends. In his words:

I had all the guys come into the team meeting room the night before for a pre-game speech. As Cedric sat in a wheelchair facing us, I asked him, "Cedric, can you tell the guys what happened?"

He told his story to the players, and talked about never giving up.

"I had dreams," Cedric said. "I had hopes. This injury doesn't change my dreams and hopes. It just changes how I'm gonna get there."

It was a real inspiration. At the end he said:

"I want you guys to know something. I get up every morning and I just know something good is going to happen to me. This morning I got up and thought, 'Now I get to speak to my favorite team. Tomorrow I get to watch you guys beat the Redskins. Monday I get my new legs.' Next time you see me, I'm going to be walking on legs."

The guys loved it, and gave him a standing ovation.

On Sunday, we won the game. (Cedric was honored during the game as he was shown on giant screens inside the stadium for the audience to applaud his service).

I gave him my phone number, and we texted once a month for almost year. He'd send pictures of his accomplishments: hiking up a mountain in Georgia, running his first half-marathon, et cetera.

Almost a year later, we were getting ready to open up our season.

"Would you mind speaking to the guys?" I asked him.

"I'd be honored," he said.

We hadn't seen him in a year. I'm anxious. I can't wait to see him. I got the team in the meeting room. That's 53 players who are on the roster, plus the 12-member practice squad, so that's 65 guys. We (the coaches) are waiting for him in a side room.

He walks through the door, and he is walking!
It was unbelievable!

He has his new legs and he's wearing a nice suit.

The team hadn't seen him yet. I got the security guy to open the back door to the meeting room. I got in front of everybody and said, "Listen guys, I have a guest speaker. I want to introduce you guys to somebody special. A year ago, he spoke before we played the Redskins. He epitomizes a lot of things in life, how you have to struggle, fight, and take on new challenges. I want to introduce you guys to Master Sergeant Cedric King."

He walks out, and the guys jump up to their feet.

Cedric has been with us ever since. It's been really cool. When he's in town, or we're near him, I get a text from him. If we have time, he'll come out. During the Super Bowl, he hung with the team. A few weeks after he finished the Boston Marathon, I asked him to speak to the team.

"Sometimes you really don't know how you impact people," he told us, sharing the story about how he was ready to give up due to pain and fatigue but kept going, and heard the two women from the medical tent tell him, "Young man, we want you to know what an inspiration you are to us. When we saw you, we told ourselves, 'If he can keep going, we can keep going. You've been our inspiration.'"

So Cedric told the team, "You have to be careful, because you don't know who's watching you, or how you inspire them."

Cedric has spoken to the team many times, including at training camp when we have 90 players. It's really cool.

I had him go into the meal room and talk to the guys, comparing the battlefield to the football field.

"When we're in a fire fight," Cedric said, "things are happening fast, like a two-minute drill for you when you have to score. Imagine your two-minute drill with bullets flying. People can die. When we do a drill, people win or lose."

When Cedric speaks, you can see his patriotism. Here's this guy who's willing to give his life for the betterment of his country for us.

His message to the team was all about the sacrifice of leadership.

First one in, last one out. He told the team:

"You feel like you've accomplished something and become a good leader if you can get those guys to follow you to where the bullets are coming from. You know you're doing something right."

That's how he got wounded. He didn't say, "Private, you go in."

He said, "Naw, this doesn't feel right. I'll go in."

He paid the price. That's who he is. He doesn't bear any grudges to anybody.

He has a way about himself that inspires people, because at no point does he feel sorry for himself. At no point does he use his injury as an excuse. He uses it as his motivator. He finds other ways to fulfill his dream.

His humility stands out. That's tremendous. His patriotism stands out. I really, truly believe everything he does because he feels it's a higher calling to be a soldier, to help protect us and better our lives.

It blows me away how humble he is. What's crazy about it is... at practice, he thanks everybody, and I'm like, "Are you kidding me? Thank you for being here!"

He deserves our admiration and respect.

There's a steadiness, a calmness, about him. When he talks and challenges you, which is what he does for our players, it makes our players think, "If Cedric can put up with what he's going through, how can I, who have two legs, ever shirk my duties as an athlete?'"

He makes people realize you can accomplish anything you want. If he can run the Boston Marathon and climb that mountain in Georgia, the world should be your oyster. You can do anything!

Cedric also set an excellent example when he brought his family to visit the team. I like to make sure our players see how you should behave around women, around your wife, and around your daughters. When he was showing them around, and being a gentleman, he set such a tremendous example for our players. He doted over the girls. It was really cool to see.

I couldn't be more pleased to have him around. He's been somebody that I've tried to model some of my leadership style with my players. I like to take credit for helping him, because he became an inspirational speaker.

I can't say enough good things about Master Sergeant Cedric King.

It still blows my mind every time I get to talk with Coach Rivera, and players such as Cam Newton. I never knew that by asking to meet the coach to make myself feel better, I would be able to contribute something positive to help my team. It creates an endless cycle of giving and receiving that just keeps getting better.

Choppin' it up with Cam Newton and the team before practice before the Panthers went to Super Bowl LI in 2016.

Talking with Coach Rivera at Fan Fest 2015.

RELATIONSHIPS LEAD TO IMPACTFUL EXPERIENCES

My very dear friend, Damon Lester, president of the National Association of Minority Automobile Dealers, has been extremely instrumental in my ability to speak to audiences across America.

Damon and I met at a conference where I was speaking about four years ago. Here's Damon's recollection of what happened. In his words:

> I met Cedric after he gave a speech about what happened to him, and how he began to walk. Like everyone who had heard Cedric for the first time, you're in shock and awe and very inspired.
>
> The stars and moon lined up that day. We spent half a day together, and I invited him to speak at our annual conference in Miami, Florida.

For two days before he spoke, Cedric mingled with my attendees, who didn't know who he was, or that he was the speaker. He fit right in. He was wearing suit pants, and not everyone knew he had no legs.

When it was time for him to speak, he walked on stage in his uniform, and everyone was saying, "Whoah!" Then he started his speech with the HBO Concert for Valor video showing First Lady Michelle Obama. Then he spoke about how he lost his legs, and how he learned to walk and run again.

As he gave his speech, people that I would never expect to shed a tear, shed a tear. We've had some very high caliber speakers at our conference. Cedric was the first person to actually move and inspire people.

When you have an opportunity to know Cedric or hear him speak, you come away with the perspective that, "Things could be a lot worse!"

We wake up every day worrying about our own issues or challenges, but he inspires you to wake up every morning feeling blessed that you can put your two feet on the floor.

He's a very strong-minded person, a very gifted person.

He's definitely a testament that when you think you can't, the power of your mind can help you do anything.

After people at the NAMAD conference heard Cedric speak, they took pictures with him. Corporations invited him to speak to their employees.

The following year, I brought him back to the NAMAD conference in Miami.

I added a 5:00 a.m. run-walk for Cedric to lead the day of his speech. About 30 people, including those who weren't typically runners, participated. Some who finished that mile and had never run before were crying.

After the run, Cedric took his legs off and showed the stubs, and talked about his life as we went for smoothies.

The experience was very therapeutic. He alleviated whatever people were worried about, whatever was ailing them, whatever problems they had. As people focused on him, they asked themselves, "If he can do it, why can't I? He doesn't complain, and I'm complaining."

The following year, we brought him back to the NAMAD conference, and nearly 60 people participated in the run, which we expanded to three miles.

Cedric doesn't run at a normal pace. He says, "I'm taking it easy," but he's running fast.

I said, "Man, you got springs on those legs. Nobody can keep up with that pace."

He also doesn't let anything stop him from enjoying life. Every year during the conference in Miami, we take a boat cruise. At one point during the cruise, I was talking with him and Kenya, when music started to play.

*"I want to get up and dance with my wife," Cedric said. No
one bothered him; no one looked at him. He was dancing with
Khieda, which was cool.*

*Whenever Cedric speaks, you feel this positivity that he shares
with everyone. He is very gifted, and I'm glad to call him a friend.*

Damon is an example of how the impressions you make on every person you meet can lead to long-lasting relationships that create win-win situations for you, that person, and all the people you can touch when you work together.

PRACTICING WHAT I PREACH — LIVE ON STAGE!

At the start of a speaking engagement at a law firm in Washington, DC, I walked across the stage, facing hundreds of people in an auditorium.

"I want to talk with you today about resilience and perseverance," I said, excited to share my story and leave them with an uplifting message about persisting through pain and overcoming obstacles. "Resilience is—"

Beeeep! Beeeeep!

My right prosthetic leg started to beep. Its battery powers the mechanical function that bends the knee. Five or six beeps means the battery only has 10 percent life remaining. This time, it beeped 15 times.

"What's that?" someone whispered.

An awkward hush fell on the crowd.

I didn't know what was going on. So, I tried to ignore it. I took another step. And the leg stopped working altogether! The battery conked out, and my leg died. It locked into a peg leg!

The uneasiness amongst the audience was palpable.

"This has never happened before," I said, "but the speech must go on."

Beeeep! Beeeeep! Beeeeep! Beeeeep! Beeeeep!

"It's not a bomb," I said. Everyone laughed, and I just kept going. I used my beeping, unbendable leg that was like dead weight on my body now, as an example of how to be resilient when you're tempted to feel ashamed, embarrassed, or disappointed.

Intestinal fortitude enabled me to fight on. You can't stop in the middle of the speech at a law firm. You cannot tell them you're resilient if you act defeated. I could have panicked. Panic never helped me before. Instead, I proceeded to demonstrate my message with my own response to a bizarre situation. I was grateful that it occurred, because it enabled me to take my public speaking to another level, by demonstrating what to do when the unexpected occurs on stage. The men and women commended my response and appreciated my message that became the best lesson of the year: Don't lose your focus!

After the speech, I went to Walter Reed, where the prosthetic technician hooked my leg up to the computer. An error message flashed: "Fail!"

"Dude, you put too many steps on this leg!" he said. "This leg expires. The battery is programmed for a set number of steps. You tapped it out!" My left prosthetic was fine; it does not have a computer or a battery because I still have the knee that I was born with.

The technician gave me a new, waterproof leg, straight out of the box, with a $30,000 knee. It requires daily maintenance, and the battery charge lasts about six days. The tough part is, what do you do when you forget? I walk so much, Khieda puts my leg charger in my bag. I am so grateful for the gift of my prosthetic legs. They don't just enable me to walk; they provide lessons that I can share to inspire others.

One more thing: the dead leg incident evolved into another tough moment, a test where I proved to myself that I refuse to ever host a pity party for Cedric King. Here's what happened: I left the speech and drove to the cashier's booth in the parking ramp. I handed a credit card to the cashier.

"Sorry, sir, we only take cash," he said.

"I don't have cash with me," I said.

"There's an ATM two blocks away," he said. "You can leave your car here and walk there."

My mind was spinning: *My leg is dead, I'm stuck in the parking ramp, and it's raining!*

I could have said, "Man, I've these prosthetics, and my leg has died — don't make me go two blocks." But I did not give him an opportunity to feel sorry for me.

In fact, I feel so strongly about this that King's Creed says: "God will not attend my pity party, so it won't happen; I refuse to feel sorry for myself."

Feeling sorry for yourself leads down the road to quitting. Think of wild animals: they never feel sorry for themselves. They channel their energy on survival, reproducing, and nurturing their young to carry on the species. So refuse to wallow in sorrow, even when you're thinking, *I've been fired; the relationship is tough; my parenting skills have gone off the cliff; the loan didn't come through.* Feeling sorry for yourself is the doorway to quitting.

For me, if I used my prosthetic legs — and the fact that one was dead! — as an excuse for pity from the parking lot attendant, that would be a cop out!

No! No! No!

Then, and always, I have to treat myself as if I have legs. As if I were like anybody else. I see myself as a conqueror of any challenge. So, I don't want anyone to cut me some slack because I have these legs. I'm going to do anything and everything in life as if I have legs. This mindset prevents me from spiraling down into that hopeless place where I think myself small and fail to execute God's huge mission for my life.

So, at the cashier's booth when he said I had to pay cash, and the ATM was two blocks away, I got out of my car, walked on a dead leg in the rain, got the cash, and solved the problem like anybody with two natural legs would do. *Bam!* Done. Maybe it hurt. I got wet. It was uncomfortable. Annoying. But rather than allow that moment to become a breaking point in my resolve to never give in, I used it as another Making Point that made me tougher, stronger, and more confident.

I have to practice what I preach. I had just given a talk on resilience. Walking in the rain to the ATM on a dead leg — that's resilience! Doing anything less than that would defeat my whole life's work. As would allowing my beeping, dying leg to stop me from giving a great speech at the law firm. That's the perfect time to persevere. The malfunctioning prosthetic was a blessing — it was a perfect moment to demonstrate perseverance while I'm talking about perseverance.

A part of me says I'm going to use that to tell a better story. We all need to look at our situations as tough, so we can triumph, and use that to tell a better story. You won't be inspiring to others if you use the cop out to let yourself off the hook. Others will let you off the hook. Refuse! Start by not letting yourself off the hook.

God blessed me with the privilege to serve as a public speaker. I am a storyteller. It's my job to tell you what happened *in spite of* what happened. That's where our power lies. Use it! Don't take the cop out. Find a solution to a seemingly impossible situation, and it will boost your confidence with a conqueror's spirit. That will enable you to tackle bigger problems with ease.

THE REAL YOU SPEAKS THE TRUTH

I never write a speech, no matter how big the event is. The Holy Spirit speaks to me — like a conduit — with unique messages for different audiences. In each case, I offer myself up to be used for this moment. Right now, I'm preparing to speak before 30,000 people at a conference.

Even for that, my only preparation is to constantly spend time studying, praying, meditating, and going to the gym. I am shedding away weakness by swimming and working out my physical body. That's how I know; I trust that God will give me the perfect words when I get in front of that audience. I've read that a lot of great speakers don't know what they're going to say until they get on stage and feel the energy of the audience.

I trusted that God would provide the words when I spoke at the Chicago Youth Summit in August of 2015. The audience included Starbucks CEO Howard Schultz, as well as the musical artists Common, T.I., and Usher. I did not study anything. Instead, I drew from the positive information that I have been studying for years; it all stirred in my spirit and came out as a poignant message that has attracted incredible relationships with Howard Schultz and Cigna CEO David Cordani.

I am living my dream as a motivational speaker at events across America. Top left: I spoke at the TedX Lizard Creek in North Carolina. Top right: Speaking at The Automotive Leadership Roundtable in Miami, Florida enabled me to meet Damon Lester, President of the National Association of Minority Automobile Dealers (NAMAD). Photo Credit: Automotive Leadership Roundtable. Bottom left: Thanks to Damon Lester, I have spoken several times at the annual NAMAD conference in Miami. Bottom right: I spoke to young people at the 100,000 Opportunities Initiative, sponsored by Howard Schultz of Starbucks, at the Los Angeles Convention Center.

Top: After speaking at the Chicago Youth Summit in August of 2015, I talked with Usher, T.I., and Howard Schultz of Starbucks. Middle: With Common, who was MC of the event. Photo credit: Rolling Out. Bottom: Khieda and me on vacation with Montel Williams at a resort in Tennessee in 2016.

Trust. It's scary. I didn't know what to say until the very moment that I was at the podium. God provided the perfect words! However, after that exhilarating moment, I fell down! My inner critic could have gone crazy on me! But I refused to allow embarrassment, humiliation, shame, or any negative feeling to rob me of the intoxicating joy of that experience.

Instead, I stayed mindful of the magic of that moment. As the Holy Spirit provides me with the right words, the messages flow out of my mouth, and I can see them electrify the men and women in front of me. I'm not boasting, because I don't take credit for what's happening.

I am simply a channel, a vessel, a tool, that God is using to amplify His words. It's not me. But I do bear witness as I become God's microphone, and people transform in front of me, as new ideas and inspiration pulse through their minds, bodies, and spirits, and they conceive new ways to act and become their best.

When my message is not scripted, and not rehearsed, it comes straight from my heart and soul. It is pure love and inspiration. And it makes an impact. A few years ago, I was invited to speak to hundreds of owners of Paul Mitchell Schools, which are one of many corporate sponsors for the Gary Sinise Foundation. I talked about how the Foundation donated our home, and provides amazing programs for veterans and wounded warriors. My speech struck such a deep chord that Winn Claybaugh, the dean of Paul Mitchell Schools scheduled me for a two-year speaking tour at all its schools. I have since spoken to cosmetologists, hair stylists, and barbers at more than 30 Paul Mitchell Schools across America.

Many of these students have experienced major barriers in life: financial struggles, single parenthood, lack of family support or encouragement to go to college, et cetera. My message about starting where you are, and using your obstacles as building blocks for a brilliant future, always excites them to examine themselves in a new way and see their infinite potential. It's amazing to watch as I pour my message over them; I can literally see it bubbling like champagne, as this newfound spiritual celebration sparkles in their eyes with new enthusiasm and hope for a better future. They start to believe in themselves, and I help them get there.

"Life speaks in the language of enthusiasm," I love to say in speeches. Then I share the quote from the author Paolo Coelho, who writes in *The Alchemist*, "There was a language in the world that everyone understood. It was the language of enthusiasm, of things accomplished with love."

That is the force that fuels my speeches, and I am so grateful to God for enabling me to serve as His transformative voice, that I literally want to bend down and kiss every stage that He enables me to speak from.

How-to Exercises

It's time to silence your inner critic so you can hear the guidance of your intuition, discover your life purpose, and take action to cultivate it. Write down the lies that your inner critic is telling you, then write the truth about yourself. For example, if you want to become a professional comedian, and your inner critic tells you that you're not funny, write about the times that you've made people double over with laughter.

My Inner Critic says:

_____

_____

_____

_____

The Truth is:

_____

_____

_____

_____

My Inner Critic says:

_____

_____

_____

_____

The Truth is:

_____

_____

_____

_____

My Inner Critic says:

_____

_____

_____

_____

The Truth is:

_____

_____

_____

_____

What demons from the past are finding a voice in your inner critic?

_____

_____

_____

_____

_____

_____

Compose a new script for your mind to silence the inner critic.

_____

_____

_____

_____

_____

_____

What are the best and worst possible outcomes when you silence your inner critic?

Write a mantra and repeat it often as an antidote to your inner critic:

Explore ways to make your inner critic inspire you.

_____

_____

_____

_____

_____

Enjoying and celebrating my family is a top priority. We've taken several vacations to Hawaii. In 2015, we visited Oahu, where we climbed Diamond Head. Top photo: me, Amari, Khieda, and Khamya in front. We returned to Waikiki Beach with the whole family in 2017. Bottom photo (left to right): Valton, my mom, Amari, Khieda's mom (Patricia Jackson-Holley), Khamya, and in front, Khieda and me.

Appendix

KING'S CREED

I face life with faith and fearlessness to	**K**eep	positive, so I can triumph over the toughest challenges.
God will not attend my pity party, so	**I**t	won't happen; I refuse to feel sorry for myself.
I persevere through even the worst pain,	**N**ow	knowing power to overcome anything.
When life pushes me down, I	**G**et	busy and flex my find-my-feet muscle to take positive action.
Whether it's sunny or stormy, I'm	**S**miling,	singing, and stepping in joy and gratitude that I'm alive and creating the best ME possible.
I take risks to better myself by finding the most	**C**ourageous	way to meet new people and work toward achieving my dreams.
I propel myself into my next success by	**R**emembering	the times I overcame obstacles, big and small.
I take the first step,	**E**xpecting	support to come.
I play a positive mental soundtrack,	**E**ncouraging	myself.
My word means everything, so I'm always	**D**oing	what I say I'm going to do.

CORRESPONDENCES

From: Cedric

To: Family

Sent: Tuesday, July 03, 2012 6:55 AM

Hey family,

I am so ready to come home. Thanks for all your prayers, we have been so blessed and favored. I know that you all play a major part in keeping us safe. There are so many scriptures that come to mind when I am out in those small villages that I know that you all are quoting and speaking over me and my platoon. Most of all I thank you for praying over my wife and two small daughters. I picture them in my mind each night as I go to sleep. My mom has ordered me to continue to speak and confess Psalm 91 each day. I must admit that I have missed a day sometimes but I speak it when I am unable read it physically. Thanks, Mom! This time of testing has truly shown me more than at any other time that prayer does work. This experience has taught me that prayer is one of the many weapons that God has given us to have dominion over this realm just as he has told us to have.

My wife has stayed in prayer throughout these two grueling deployments and has been a real soldier and the love of my life. I love you, babe! Well gotta get back to work now. I love you all so much, thanks for being a one of a kind family that loves and supports so unconditionally!

Love Cedric

On Tue, Jul 3, 2012 at 2:38 PM, Awesome God Bookstore [Mom] wrote:

Hi Son,

I miss you too. I read your email to Dad & Mother and they, like us, will be glad when you get home from over there, but remember: we will continue to keep you & your family in prayer. Every time I hear some unpleasant news on the TV, I again speak Psalm 91 over you, Khieda & the girls. God is so good and we are so thankful for His blessings.

Love you, son

Mom

From: cedric king
Sent: Wednesday, July 04, 2012 5:47 AM
To: Awesome God Bookstore [Mom]

We are spiritual beings in this earth having physical experiences, not the other way around. This might all sound a little crazy but I am in deep meditation about this and other subjects that I will one day share with humanity and help make the world a better place. I love you mom! see you when I get home.

Psalm 91

My mom gave Psalm 91 to me before my deployment. Its significance
to me: the placement of my feet; the knowledge that every step would
be guided; that every step was perfectly designed; and maybe every
step was ordered by God.

PSALM 91

Whoever dwells in the shelter of the Most High
will rest in the shadow of the Almighty.
I will say of the Lord, "He is my refuge and my fortress,
my God, in whom I trust."
Surely he will save you
from the fowler's snare
and from the deadly pestilence.
He will cover you with his feathers,
and under his wings you will find refuge;
his faithfulness will be your shield and rampart.
You will not fear the terror of night,
nor the arrow that flies by day,
nor the pestilence that stalks in the darkness,
nor the plague that destroys at midday.
A thousand may fall at your side,
ten thousand at your right hand,

but it will not come near you.

You will only observe with your eyes

and see the punishment of the wicked.

If you say, "The Lord is my refuge,"

and you make the Most High your dwelling,

no harm will overtake you,

no disaster will come near your tent.

For he will command his angels concerning you

to guard you in all your ways;

they will lift you up in their hands,

so that you will not strike your foot against a stone.

You will tread on the lion and the cobra

you will trample the great lion and the serpent.

"Because he loves me," says the Lord, "I will rescue him;

I will protect him, for he acknowledges my name.

He will call on me, and I will answer him;

I will be with him in trouble,

I will deliver him and honor him.

With long life I will satisfy him

and show him my salvation."

Biography

MASTER SERGEANT CEDRIC KING (Ret.) entered the United States Army in 1995. During a career that took him from an infantry private to a position of leadership in the elite Rangers, King graduated from a number of distinguished Army schools. These included the United States Army Jumpmaster School, United States Army Pathfinder School, Air Assault School, the United States Army Ranger School, and others. He is the recipient of the Bronze Star, the Purple Heart, the Meritorious Service Medal, and is a four-time Best Ranger Competition participant.

On July 25, 2012, during his second tour in Afghanistan, King was severely injured by an improvised explosive device. The blast caused major internal injuries, permanent loss to part of his right arm and hand, and the amputation of both legs. He applied the same determined, can-do mindset to his recovery that he had relied on to succeed as an elite Army Ranger. With the love and support of his wife Khieda and daughters Amari and Khamya, he began rebuilding his life.

Just 21 months after losing both legs, King completed the Boston Marathon, running on prosthetic blades. He has gone on to compete in a number of physically daunting events, including a 70.3-mile half Ironman Triathlon, the 2014 New York City Marathon, and the 48.6-mile Disney Marathon series. There, he successfully completed four runs in four days — a 5K, 10K, half marathon, and full marathon. King shares his inspirational story of endurance with audiences across the country, including schools, churches, the National Football League, and Fortune 500 companies. Just as he led and motivated men in combat, he now leads and motivates others to see the possibilities in their own lives.

Index

How You Can Engage with Cedric

Faith. Family. Focus.

The Cedric King Team

6600 Sugarloaf Parkway, Suite 400

Duluth, GA 30097

info@TheCedricKingTeam.com

www.TheCedricKingTeam.com

Connect with Us on

Facebook https://www.facebook.com/cedric.king.336

Twitter https://twitter.com/cedricking10

Instagram https://www.instagram.com/cedricking2/

LinkedIn https://www.linkedin.com/in/cedrickingmsg/

The Kings: Amari, Khieda, Khamya, and Cedric. Photo Credit: Kent Horner.